rather*austin*

eat. shop. explore > discover local gems

researched, photographed and written by currie person, elizabeth winslow and kaie wellman

toc

neighborhoods

- p.09 **downtown > 2nd street district**
- p.23 **downtown > clarksville**
- p.41 **east austin**
- p.67 **midtown > ut / the drag**
- p.85 **midtown > hyde park**
- p.95 **north austin**
- p.129 **south austin**
- p.179 **etc.**

EAT

antonelli's cheese shop
apna bazaar
barley swine
casey's new orleans snowballs
chen's noodle house
chosun galbi
contigo
counter cafe
dai due
east end wines
east side king at the liberty bar
east side showroom
el caribe
el meson taqueria
el naranjo
farmhouse delivery
foreign & domestic
franklin barbecue
gourdough's
g'raj mahal cafe
haddingtons
home slice pizza
hotel san josé lounge
justine's brasserie
la boîte
la condesa
little deli
lucky's puccias
lulu b's
musashino sushi dokoro
odd duck farm to trailer
olivia
owl tree roasting
panaderia chuy
perla's seafood & oyster bar
salt & tiime
sambet's cajun deli & firey foods store
smitty's market
tâm deli & cafe
texas french bread
the backspace
uchi/uchiko
whip in
yellow jacket social club

SHOP

12th street books
alyson fox / a small collection
austin bike farm
bell and bird
bows + arrows
breakaway records
by george men
by george women
catbird paper
complete clothing
dog and pony
domy books
feathers
fiddler's green music shop
ga ga
gene rogers optical
helm
howl interiors
kick pleat
laced with romance
loretta flower
mercury design studio
miss natalie
mod green pod
moss
nick kicks
roadhouse rags
rootin' ridge toymakers
schatzelein
spartan
spruce
stag
stitch lab
switched on
the corner shoppe mall
tiny's western shop
trailer space records
underwear
uptown modern
w3ll people

notes about austin

rather *austin* EDITORS >

Currie Person's experience as a feature film location scout honed her taste for exquisite design detail. **Spartan**, her shop in Austin, is a tightly edited collection of beautiful and functional objects.

Elizabeth Winslow is a chef, writer, committed locavore and seasoned forager. She is a partner in **Farmhouse Delivery**, an all-local grocery delivery service in Austin.

Kaie Wellman is the creator of the *eat.shop guides* and *rather*. She likes nothing better than traipsing around a city peering into its nooks and crannies. though a lover of pretty objects and fine food, Kaie loves puffy down vests and donuts.

Note from Kaie > Over the last 6 years, I authored all three of the *eat.shop austin* books and loved just about every hot, sweaty minute of doing so. I don't know what it is about this town, but I haven't been able to get enough of it. Maybe it's taking a dip in Barton Springs pool at 9pm on a steamy night or creating a food pyramid out of barbeque and snowcones? Or is it that special breed of Austin storyteller that has me in the palm of their hand with every far-fetched story told? Whatever it is about this place, I'd like to bottle it up and sell it. I'd be a bazillionaire. I'm now passing the **rather** mantle over to Currie and Elizabeth, two incredible Austinites who will expand on the Austin experience for years to come.

And if you need a break from eating and shopping, here are some ideas for you:

1 > Float on Lady Bird Lake: Experiencing the water culture around Austin is key, and one of the best ways to do this is to rent a canoe or a kayak. There are plenty of companies to rent from like .zilkerboats.com or rowingdock.com

2 > SXSW: Though it's long away from being the little festival that could, South By is still a barrel o' fun that not only includes music and film, but also interactive exhibits. Come for one, come for all. It's guaranteed that something will launch here that the rest of the world will be talking about down the line. sxsw.com

3 > Visit an Urban Farm: Austin has more farms within its city limits (many in East Austin) than any other city of its size in the United States. Though most aren't open to the public, others are like Boggy Creek Farm and Green Gate Farms are open on limited days or have farm stands. boggycreekfarm.com / greengatefarms.com

4 > Live Music: If you come to this town and you don't go see some type of live music, you are stark raving mad. Just pick up a Chronicle and point your finger at something and go.

it's all about...

exploring locally

*discovering a sense of place
behind the veneer of a city*

*experiencing what gives
a city its soul through its
local flavor*

rather EVOLUTION

If you are thinking that this book looks suspiciously like an *eatshop guide*, you're on to something. As of October 2011, the *eatshop guides* evolved into **rather** to give readers a more vibrant experience when it comes to local eating and shopping. It's all about what you'd **rather** be doing with your time when you explore a city—eat at a chain restaurant or an intimate little trattoria devouring dishes the chef created from farm fresh ingredients? You get the idea.

USING **rather**

All of the businesses featured in this book are first and foremost locally owned, and they are chosen to be featured because they are utterly authentic and uniquely conceived. And since this isn't an advertorial guide, there's no money exchanging hands • Make sure to double check the hours of the business before you go, as many places change their hours seasonally • The pictures and descriptions for each business are meant to give a feel for a place, but please know those items may no longer be available • Our maps are stylized, meaning they don't show every street • Small local businesses have always had to work that much harder to keep their heads above water, and not all the businesses featured will stay open. Please go to the **rather** website for updates • **rather** editors research, shoot and write everything you see in this book • Only natural light is used to shoot and there's no styling or propping

restaurants >
$ = inexpensive $$ = medium $$$ = expensive

Go to **rather.com** to learn more

where to lay your weary head

for more hotel choices, visit >

austinhotels.net

TravelShark

PART OF THE TRAVELSHARK TRAVEL NETWORK

hotel san josé
1316 south congress avenue (south austin)
512.852.2350 / sanjosehotel.com
standard double from $160 suites from $335
bar: hotel san josé lounge coffee and light snacks: jo's (next door)
notes: legendarily cool austin hotel

w hotel austin
200 lavaca street (downtown)
512.542.3600 / starwoodhotels.com
standard double from $275
notes: the w brings its signature style to austin

four seasons austin
98 san jacinto boulevard (downtown)
512.478.4500 / fourseasons.com/austin
standard double from $350
restaurant: trio
notes: it's elegant, it has a spa and it sits on the banks of lady bird lake

kimber modern
110 the circle (south austin)
512.912.1046 / kimbermodern.com
standard double from $250
notes: a small, modern hotel with the intimacy of a bed and breakfast

hotel saint cecilia
112 academy drive (south austin)
512.852.2400 / hotelsaintcecilia.com
studios from $295 suites from $490
notes: a secluded estate

more local gems

these businesses appeared in previous editions of eat.shop austin

EAT

amy's ice cream
anderson's coffee co.
arkie's grill
big top candy shop
boggy creek farm
caffe medici
carousel lounge
chez nous
clay pit
daily juice
dart bowl steakhouse
din ho chinese bbq
dirty martin's place
east side cafe
east side pies
el chile
el chilito
enoteca
flip happy crepes
fonda san miguel
foodheads
frisco shop
good pop
hong kong supermarket inc
home slice pizza
hoover's cooking
house park bar-be-que
hut's hamburgers
jade leaves teahouse
jeffrey's
jim-jim's water ice
jo's
juan in a million
koriente
la cocina de consuelo
lamberts
la mexicana bakery
little city
mean-eyed cat
mrs. johnson's bakery
nau's enfield pharmacy
p. terry's
phil's icehouse
phoenicia bakery & deli
polvos
portabla
progress coffee
quality seafood market
rosita's al pastor
sandy's frozen custard
sasha's gourmet russian market
sno-beach hawaiian shaved ice
sunflower
taco deli
teo
the woodland
the original hauffbrau
thom's market
tiniest bar in texas
top notch
torchy's tacos
vespaio
victory grill
wiggy's

SHOP

allens boots
amelia's retro vogue & relics
aviary
betty sport
big bertha's
blackbird
blackmail
dart bowl pro shop
eliza page
end of an ear
finch
habana house
hem
if+d
martinez brothers taxidermist
milk+honey
nest modern
quincy's guitars
sabia
roadhouse relics
room service vintage
ruth's pinata land
service
solid gold
terra toys
tesoros
texas custom boots
texas state surplus facility
the lightbulb shop
toy joy
uncommon objects
upstairs downstairs
verbena floral design
whetstone audio
yard dog

notes

downtown

2nd street district

eat

e01 dai due
e02 el naranjo
e03 g'raj mahal
e04 la condesa
e05 the backspace

shop

s01 mercury design

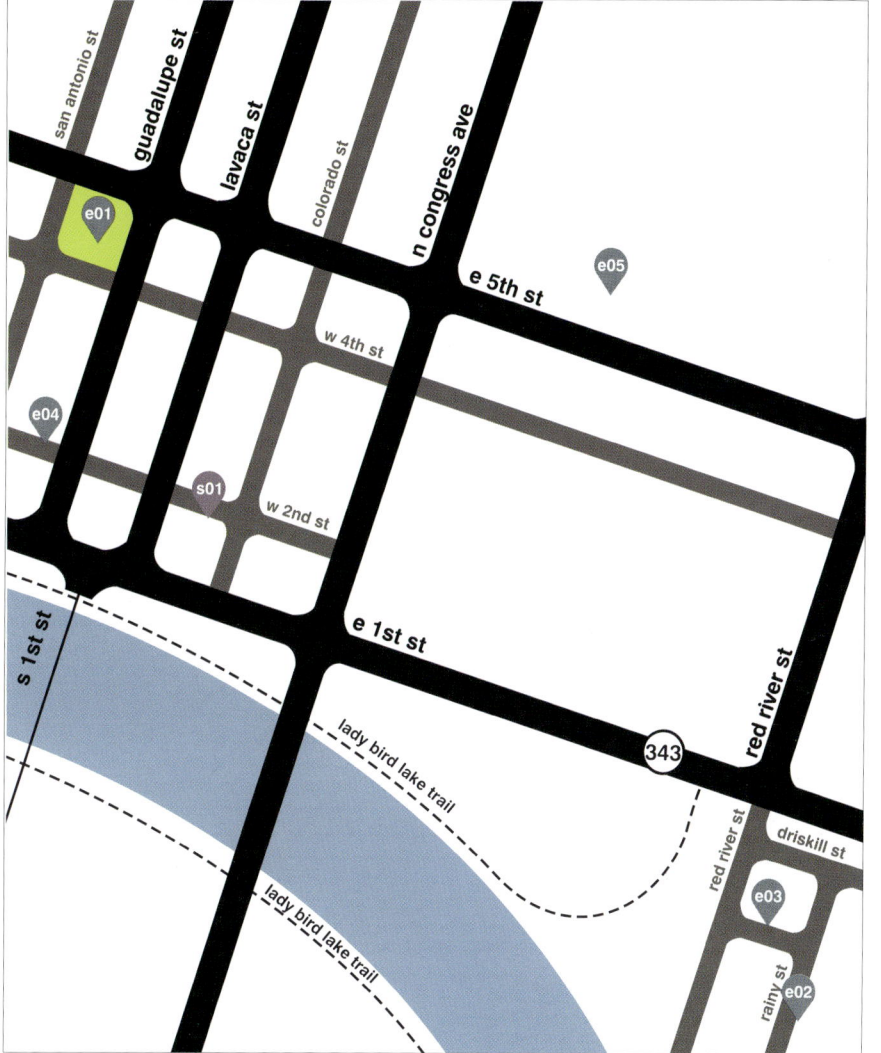

dai due

roving butcher shop and supper club

Austin Farmers' Market
Republic Square Park at 4th and Guadalupe
(Downtown) *map E01*
512.524.0688
www.daidueaustin.net

twitter @daidue
sat 9a - 1p
supper club. butcher shop. classes
$-$$ first come, first served

Yes. Please: *fresh bloody mary mix, wild boar & pepper sausage, bockwurst, boudin blanc, jujube paste, rabbit & olive oil rillettes, southern style pickles*

Unless you are a hardcore vegan/vegetarian or you're living under a rock, I'm sure you are aware that a trend of meat, meat and more meat has been sweeping the country for a while now. Within this newfound love for pork belly and trotters are folks who are embracing the artisanal craft of meat curing and butchering. The couple behind **Dai Due** is a great example. Austinites flock to their farmers' market stand not just for meat products but also for their inspired condiments. And if this isn't enough **Dai Due** for you, then book a seat at one of their beloved supper clubs and embrace the deliciousness.

el naranjo

traditional mexican cuisine served out of a truck

85 Rainey Street
Near Red River (Downtown) *map E02*
512.474.2776
www.elnaranjo-restaurant.com

twitter @elnaranjoaustin
mon - sat 5 - 10p
dinner
$-$$ first come, first served

Yes, Please: *sangria señorial, hibiscus iced tea, veracruzanos molotes, empanadas de hongos, cochinita pibil tostadas, chileajo tacos, de garnachas*

I'm not sure this is something I want to admit publicly, but I'm all about telling the truth, so here it goes—I don't really like mole. There, it's out. I feel so much better. But now that I've fessed up, **El Naranjo** comes along and confuses me, because not only do I like Iliana's moles, I think I might love them. She features a number of traditional Oaxacan moles as specials ranging from a verde to manchamanteles (which translates to "tablecloth stainer"), which is made from dried chilies, charred tomatoes and ripe fruit. Just the description makes me drool.

g'raj mahal cafe

fresh, organic indian fare

91 Red River
Entrance on Davis (Downtown) *map E03*
512.480.2255
www.grajmahalcafe.com

tue - thu 5p - midnight fri - sat 5p - 3a
dinner
$$ reservations accepted

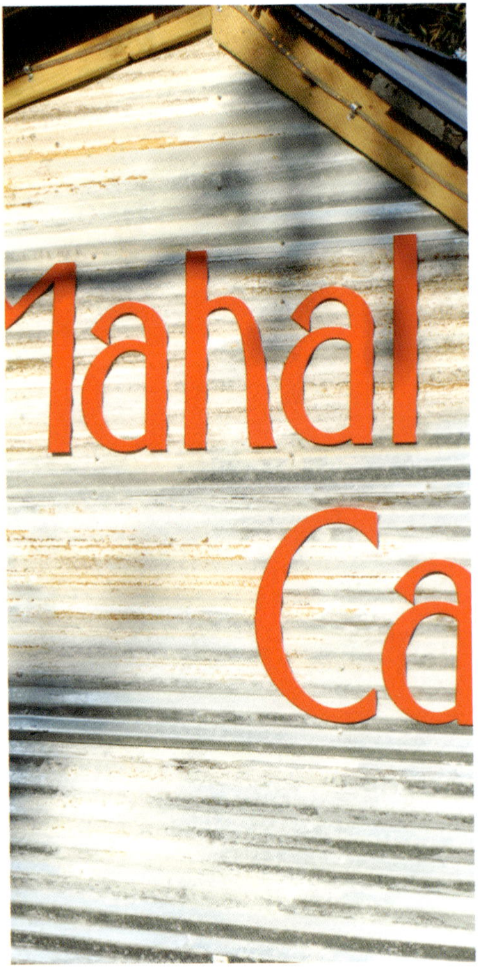

Yes. Please: *rose lassi, chai, curried lamb samosa, papri chat, shrimp tikka masala, baingan bartha, lamb tikka, indian beignets*

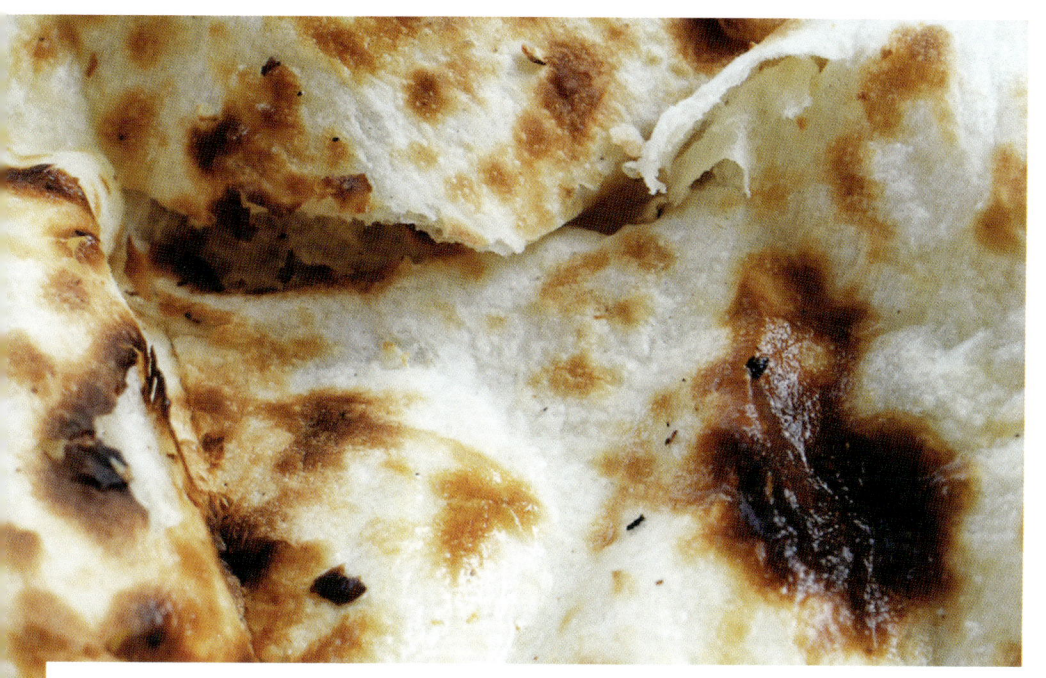

Just to prove to you how mindless I can be while in the midst of the production of these books, it didn't occur to me until visiting here a couple of times that the way to pronounce **G'Raj Mahal** is Garage Mahal. Word play. Right. Got it. Now that I've got the pronunciation right, I can talk about how I think this is one of the great spots in Austin to spend a warm night. Bring a bunch of friends, some crisp white wine or cold Tiger beer and order this delicious Indian food family style. Then settle in for an incredibly pleasant night amongst the backdrop of the sculptural, skeletal bikes of the **Austin Bike Zoo**.

la condesa

vivacious, mexico city-inspired cuisine

400 West Second Street
Corner of Guadalupe (Downtown) *map E04*
512.499.0300
www.lacondesaaustin.com

twitter @lacondesaaustin
see website for hours
brunch. dinner
$$ reservations accepted

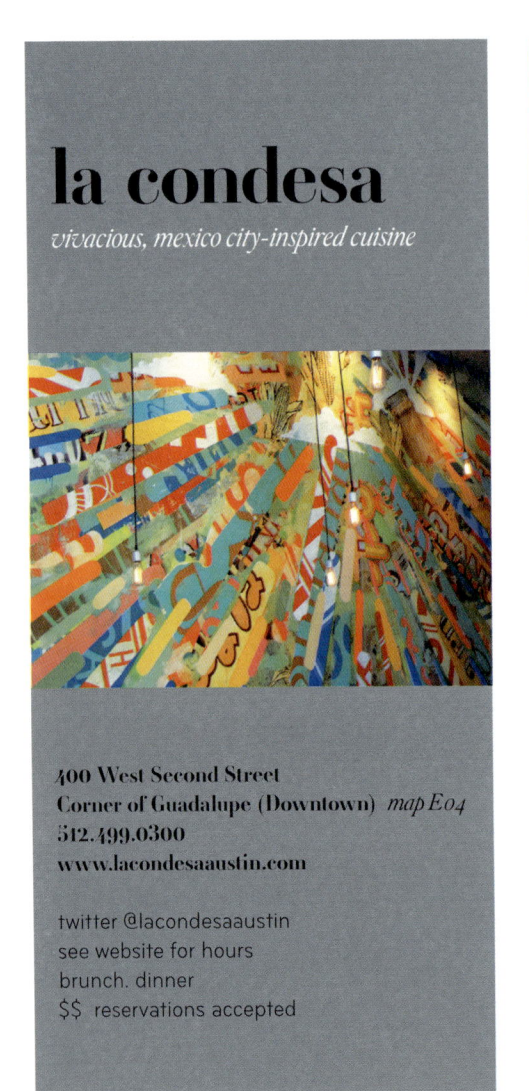

Yes, Please: *el cubico, over 80 varieties of tequila, hamachi ceviche, atun tostada, calabaza, pollo dominguero, costillos de puerco, spicy boca negra*

Something about imaginary cities appeals to me more than the real thing. The Paris and New York of my dreams are filled with alluring little side streets dotted with boutiques and bistros that I will sadly never find in real life. I also have an imaginary Mexico City that is boisterous, colorful and filled with mind numbingly good food. This description could also fit **La Condesa**, which is inspired by the incredible food culture of MC, from its street fare to its cantinas. The scene here has a spark to it, the décor is vibrant and the food is as pretty to look at as it is delicious to eat. And the best part is that **La Condesa** is real.

mercury design studio
vivid lifestyle and home design store

209 West Second Street
Near Colorado (Downtown) *map S01*
512.236.0100
www.mercurydesignstudio.com

mon - sat 10a - 7p sun 11a - 6p
custom orders / design services

Yes, Please: *reinvintage: house line of repurposed furniture, john derian, taschen books, seda france, geode jewelry, niven morgan, jonathon adler*

Though I'm a happy person, I like the color gray. I love heather gray clothing. I think dove gray walls are chic. My favorite color of car is charcoal gray. Something about this gray fixation makes me worry that I'm secretly dour or soon to be heading that way. To make sure this doesn't happen, I'm heading to **Mercury Design Studio** to get my color fix. Walking in here is energizing. Every corner tells a different color story, each more vibrant than the last. Owner Steve Shuck not only mixes tones, he mixes products: reworked vintage furniture to luscious scarves to unusual jewelry. Color me happy.

the backspace

authentic neapolitan-style pizza

507 San Jacinto Street
Between 5th and 6th (Downtown) *map E05*
512.474.9899
www.thebackspace-austin.com

twitter @backspaceaustin
daily 5 - 11p
dinner
$-$$ reservations recommended

Yes, Please: *a good chianti, prosciutto wrapped mozzarella, cauliflower caponata, pizza bianca, fennel sausage pizza, hazelnut chocolate budino*

There are ovens... and then there are $12,000 custom-built ovens shipped straight from Naples, Italy that heat up to 900 degrees and blast a circle of dough into perfectly charred, chewy and crispy Neapolitan pizza nirvana in just 90 seconds. Chef/owner Shawn Cirkiel thrills to the challenge of producing everything on the restaurant's perfectly-curated menu from just that oven. Wood-fired sides, salads and appetizers round out the offerings, along with a lovely and affordable list of Italian wines and microbrews. You've gotta love it—no stove, no range, no puny convection oven in-house. Just a man, his Cirigliano oven and perfect pizza.

downtown

clarksville

eat

e06 counter cafe
e07 haddingtons
e08 lucky's puccias

shop

s02 12th street books
s03 by george men
s04 by george women
s05 kick pleat
s06 underwear

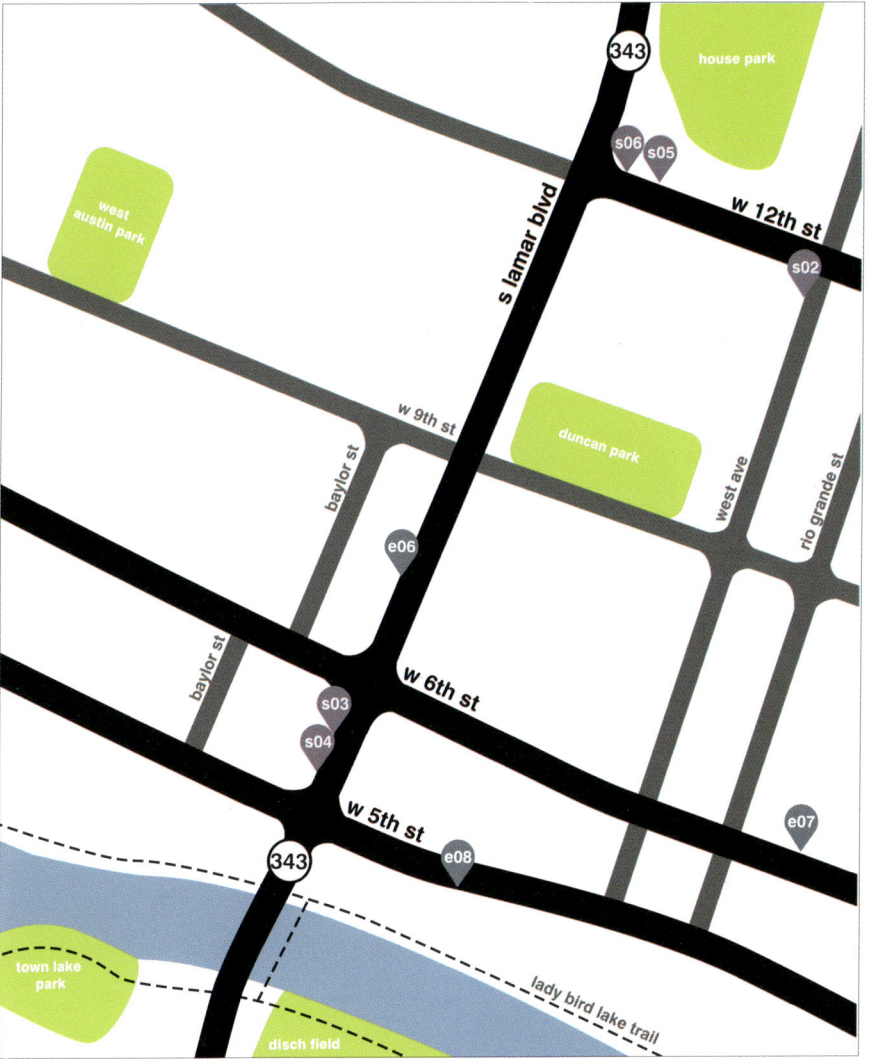

12th street books

antiquarian books

827 West 12th Street
Between Shoal Creek and West Avenue
(Downtown) *map S02*
512.499.8828
www.12thstreetbooks.com

mon - fri by chance or by appointment
sat 10a - 6p
online shopping. book appraisals

Yes, Please: *"agee on film"* by james agee, *"hornblower and the hotspur"* by c.s. forester, *"les diners de gala"* by salvador dali, *"marcel ducham"* by octavio paz

The saying "can't see the forest for the trees" certainly pertains to my overlooking **12th Street Books** for years while scouring this town. It's not that I didn't love this antiquarian/vintage bookstore, it's that I never saw it. Over the years, I've driven up and down this street zillions of times, but somehow this cloaked gem was hidden from my view. And oh what I was missing—a den-like space full of gently aged treasures of the written word and sumptuously illustrated art books. I could have easily spent all day in here, but now that it's on my radar, returning over and over again will be a breeze.

by george men
sharp men's fashion

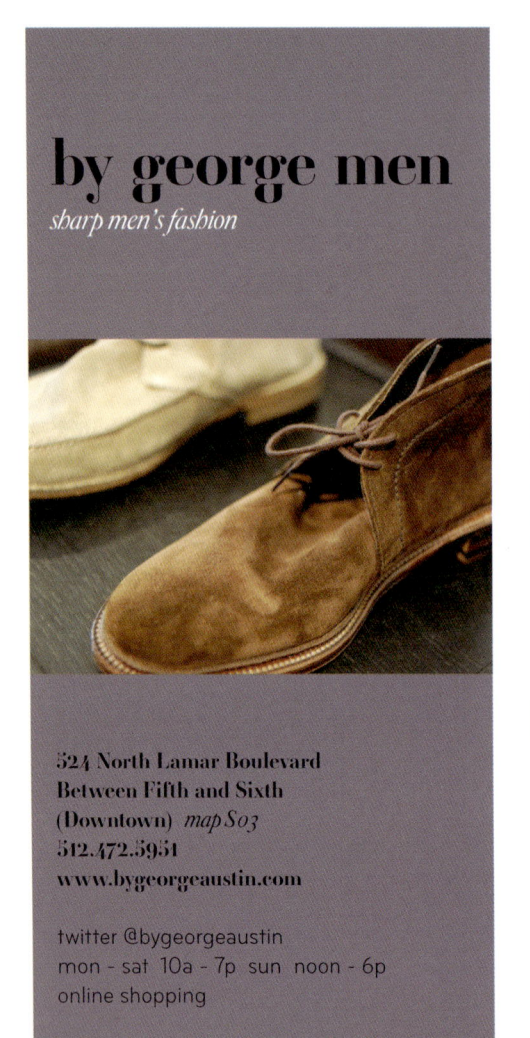

524 North Lamar Boulevard
Between Fifth and Sixth
(Downtown) *map S03*
512.472.5951
www.bygeorgeaustin.com

twitter @bygeorgeaustin
mon - sat 10a - 7p   sun noon - 6p
online shopping

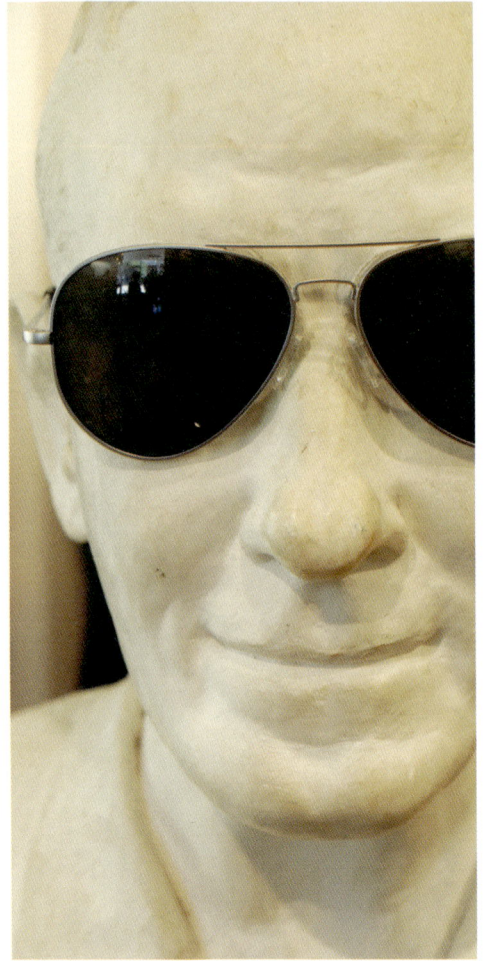

Yes. Please: *levi's xx, golden goose, porter bags, post overalls, billy reid, simon miller, maison martin margiela, lanvin*

Since 2008, stories in the media about the state of retail have been nothing but bad news. It got to the point where it was just too depressing to pick up a newspaper. So when The New York Times went looking for a positive story in conjunction to retail, it's no surprise they chose **By George**. Matthew and Katy Culmo are retailer extraordinaires and know how to roll with the punches. In the midst of the dirge, they reintroduced men's clothing, which is fantastic because Matthew is a menswear expert. Everything here is not only fashionably sharp, it's also totally wearable. Perfect for Austin.

by george women

sharp women's fashion

524 North Lamar Boulevard
Between Fifth and Sixth
(Downtown) *map S04*
512.472.5951
www.bygeorgeaustin.com

twitter @bygeorgeaustin
mon - sat 10a - 7p sun noon - 6p
online shopping

Yes. Please: *nili lotan, dosa, hazel brown, gary graham, raquel allegra, zero+ maria cornejo, coclico, current/elliott*

I think Katy Culmo and I are the middle-aged version of the Olsen twins. We aren't related, but we look a bit alike, are the same not-so-tall height (don't say short, please) and have a similar style of dressing. When I'm walking around looking at the women's clothing at **By George** with her and she notes pieces she is drawn to, it's on the tip of my tongue to say how much I like the same, whether the piece is drop-dead elegant or casually simple. She understands fashion is not something meant to make you slavish or turn you into a Stepford; it's to have fun with, whatever your budget looks like. That's right, sister.

counter cafe

a modern diner

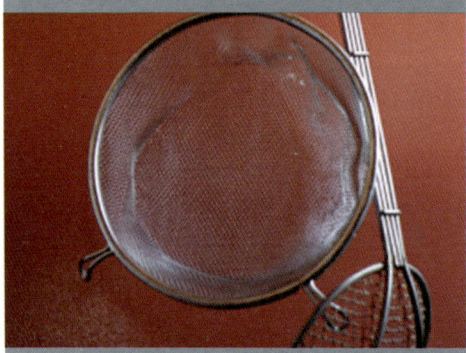

626 North Lamar Boulevard
Corner of Seventh (Downtown) *map E06*
512.708.8800
www.countercafe.com

daily 8a - 4p
breakfast. lunch
$-$$ first come, first served

Yes, Please: *counter michelada, bellinis, breakfast tacos, counter benedict, texas quail & eggs, the famous pimiento cheese sandwich*

I like breakfast well enough, though there are certain things that appeal to me on a menu that aren't that great when going down the old gullet. I find that steak and eggs falls into this category. I like steak. I like eggs. But when I get tempted to eat them together for breakfast it falls into the category of way. too. damn. much. food. But **Counter Cafe's** quail and eggs is just right and so darn Texan. I think the perfectly grilled split quail and a couple of perfectly fried eggs is a great. way. to. start. your. day.

haddingtons

an american tavern

601 West 6th Street
Between Rio Grande and Nueces
(Downtown) *map E07*
512.992.0187
www.haddingtonsrestaurant.com

twitter @haddingtons
see website for hours
brunch. lunch. dinner
$$-$$$ reservations recommended

Yes, Please: *old speckled hen bitter ale, duck fat sazerac, grilled quail risotto, pickled baby lamb's tongue salad, chilled buttermilk and sweet pea soup*

Austin is full of live music venues and hip bars, but quietly elegant and homey pubs with award-winning, world-class bartenders and exquisitely prepared food? Not so much. Enter **Haddingtons**, with a fantasy English pub interior designed by architect Michael Hsu and drinks designed by classically-trained mixologists. Think dark nooks and secret spaces inside the restaurant's warren of rooms. Chef Jimmy Corwell's lighter than your average pub-grub rustic cuisine honors the tradition of the classic tavern but goes down well- along with an expertly-mixed Sazerac or two—in a modern American city.

kick pleat

clothing you want to wear

918 West 12th Street
Near Lamar (Downtown) *map S05*
512.445.4500
www.kickpleat.com

mon - sat 10a - 6p sun 1 - 5p
online shopping

Yes. Please: *hache, rachel comey, a piece apart, sofie d'hoore, humanoid, acne, ld tuttle, soulita bags*

It's been six years now since I wrote the first Austin book, and I have met most of the owners of the businesses that are featured except Wendi Koletar, the owner of **Kick Pleat**. I was convinced there was no Wendi but instead a mysterious person with a great sense of style, constantly rumored to be in Paris or some other exotic locale. She became the Banksy of the Austin retail scene to me. But then someone professing to be Wendi introduced herself to me last year in NYC. This woman certainly looked chic, sporting the signature **Kick Pleat** modern yet highly wearable wardrobe. Was it Wendi? Who knows.

lucky's puccias

rustic puglian sandwiches

817 West 5th Street
Between Bowie and West
(Downtown) *map E08*
512.739.8785

twitter @luckyspuccias
lunch tue - sun 11a - 2p
dinner wed 6:30 - 10:30p thu 7p - 12a
fri - sat 7p - 1a sun 6 - 8p
lunch. dinner
$ first come, first served

Yes, Please: *wood-fired sandwiches > the lucky, the contadina, the arrostita*

I'm a sandwich snob. You can keep your lackluster subs and sad little hamburgers. I expect bread to be freshly baked, spreads to be handmade and applied with a light hand, and fillings to be inventive, crisp and expertly layered. Lucky, a recent émigré from Puglia, understands such exacting standards. He wakes early each day to bake his puccias (yeasty soft rolls with a crackly crust) in a wood burning oven and to mix up small batches of the basil and chili oils and the artichoke pesto that will dress his sandwiches. What did we do in Austin to deserve these earthy, rustic, in-every-way-perfect sandwiches? Don't ask questions, just count yourself lucky and puccia mouth on it.

underwear

luscious lingerie

916B West 12th Street
Near Lamar (Downtown) *map S06*
512.478.1515
www.shop-underwear.com

twitter @shopunderwear
mon - sat 10a - 6p noon 1 - 5p
online shopping. registries. special orders

Yes, Please: *mimi holliday, stella mccartney, blush, eberjey, myla, the lake and stars, huit, jimmy jane*

What is it with people wanting to go commando? I just recently spent an otherwise perfectly nice night with friends that was sullied with all the talk of commando-ism. I'm pretty sure if these gals shop at **Underwear**, this picadillo will go out the window. The underthings here are just so pretty, with everything from super romantic boudoir lingerie to everyday bras and panties. And lest you worry about looking like a Pussycat Doll, know that owner Elizabeth Tigar buys incredibly fashion forward lines that are both tasteful and sexy. So ladies, put your panties back on and get yourself some **Underwear**.

east austin

eat

e09 contigo
e10 east side wines
e11 east side king at the liberty bar
e12 east side showroom
e13 franklin barbecue
e14 justine's brasserie
e15 owl tree roasting
e16 yellow jacket social club

shop

s07 domy books
s08 helm
s09 switched on
s10 trailer space records

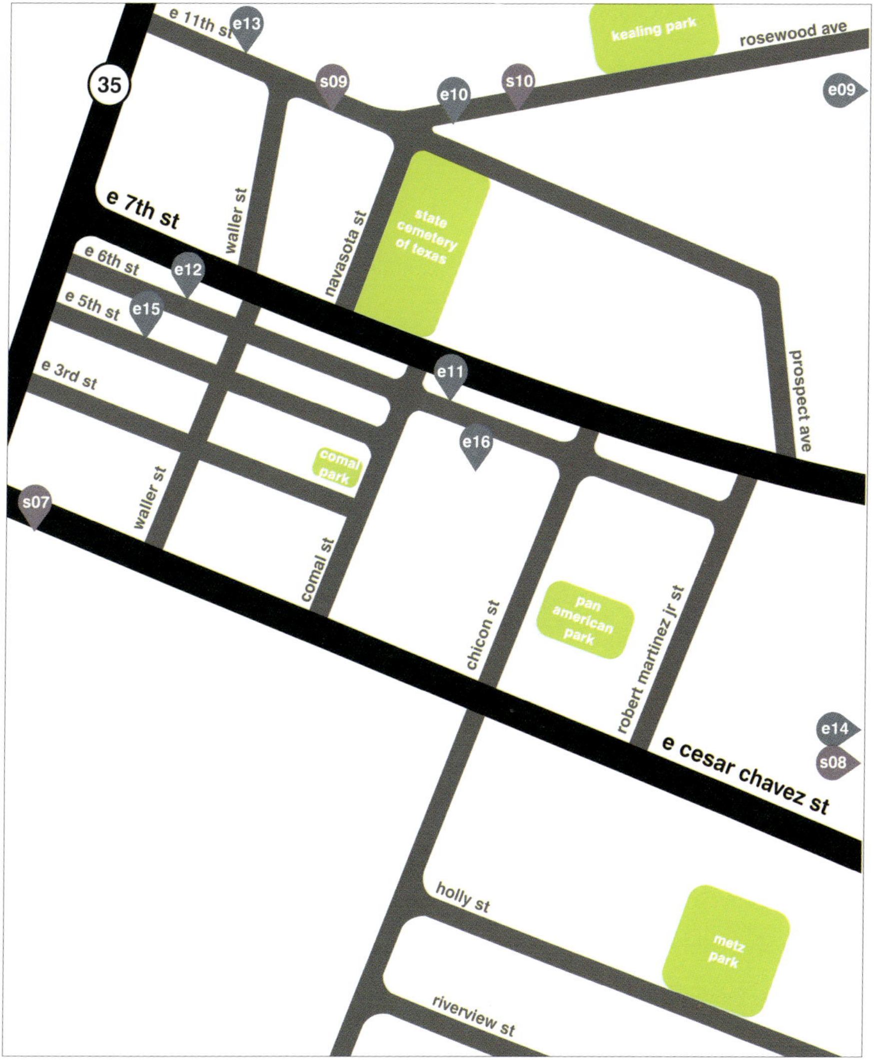

e 11th st
e13
kealing park
rosewood ave
35
s09
e10
s10
e09
e 7th st
waller st
navasota st
state cemetery of texas
e 6th st
e12
e 5th st
e15
prospect ave
e 3rd st
e11
e16
comal park
s07
waller st
comal st
chicon st
pan american park
robert martinez jr st
e14
s08
e cesar chavez st
holly st
metz park
riverview st

contigo
bringing the best from the ranch to the city

WELCOME to CONTIGO please sit ANYWHERE

2027 Anchor Lane
Between Manor and Airport
(East Austin) *map E09*
512.614.2260
www.contigotexas.com

twitter @contigoaustin
sun - fri 5p - midnight sat noon - 12a
dinner
$$ first come, first served

Yes, Please: *contigo ranch swizzle, el pepino cocktail, rabbit & dumplings, pigs in a blanket, baby octopus with cherry tomatoes & chili broth*

Few people know that besides being the Live Music Capital of the World, Austin also happens to be the alfresco eating and swilling capital of the world. The stars at night and all that, right? Austin's almost-year-round lovely weather and fond memories of childhood hunting trips, weekend retreats, cattle roundups, and barbecues at his family's Contigo Ranch inspired owner Ben Edgerton to create an open-air space with a laid back vibe that begs you to implore the friendly waitstaff to keep those ranch-inspired small plates coming.

rather.com 43

domy books
progressive things to read

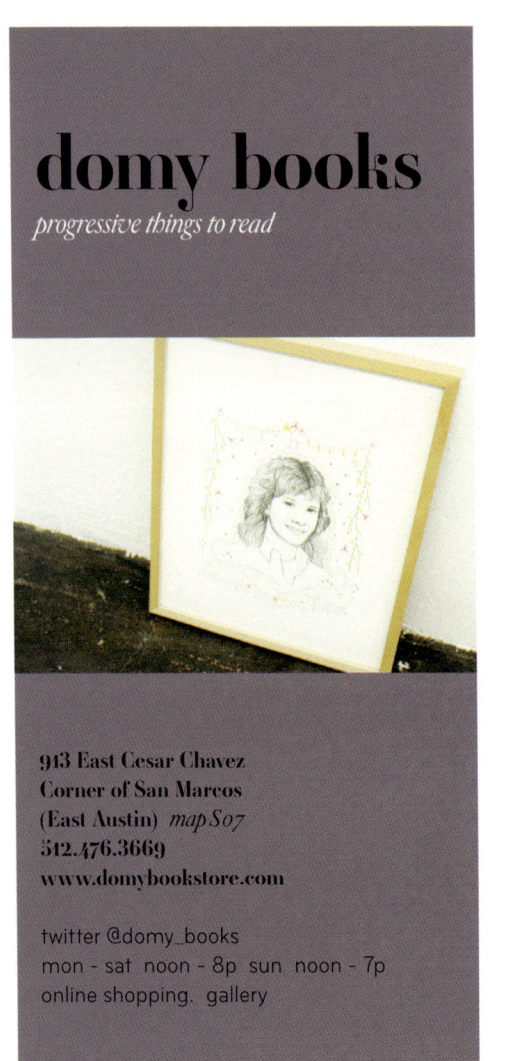

913 East Cesar Chavez
Corner of San Marcos
(East Austin) *map S07*
512.476.3669
www.domybookstore.com

twitter @domy_books
mon - sat noon - 8p sun noon - 7p
online shopping. gallery

Yes, Please: *the complete film works by robert frank, "tiny art director" by bill zeman, "shovel in a hole" by urs fischer, mags & zines, apocalypse cakes recipe cards*

I love books, which you might have guessed because I'm a publisher. But to be more specific, though I love many different genres of books, I have special feelings for art books. I could get all print-geeky on you and talk about how the interaction of ink on paper is infinitely intriguing to me, but I'll focus more on the base level of attraction: art books are beautiful to look at, and **Domy Books** is filled with the most eclectic, titillating collection in Austin. If I went MIA in this town, the first place someone should look for me is here amongst the stacks, happily reading away.

rather.com 45

east end wines

a great bottle shop

1209 Rosewood Avenue
Corner of 11th (East Austin) *map E10*
512.904.9056
www.eastendwinesatx.com

twitter @eastendwines
mon - wed 10a - 7p thu - sat 10a - 8p
$-$$ first come, first served

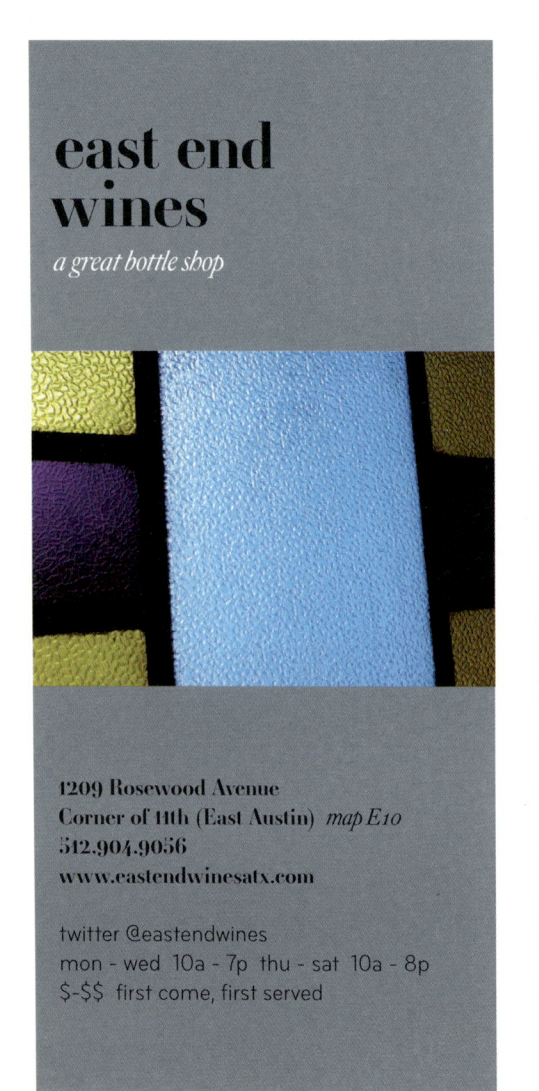

Yes, Please: *'08 becker vineyards prairie rotie, '08 block nine pinot noir caiden's vineyard, tru organic gin, dripping springs vodka, unibroue la fin du monde beer*

Everybody has secret wishes. I wish I had longer legs, thicker hair, and that I had a more refined palate when it comes to wine. For example, I would love to be able to define the difference between a Pinot Noir and a Gamay, or be able to connect a wine to its producer just by the way it tastes. I think my only hope is to have the knowledgeable **East End Wines** staff help me out. Owner Mike Miller and his crew obviously know their stuff, and even when helping out a wine challenged person like myself, they make the complex world of vino much easier to navigate. Cheers to them!

rather.com 47

east side king at the liberty bar

asian-inspired drinking sustenance

1618 East Sixth Street
Between Comal and Chalmers
(East Austin) *map E11*
512.422.5884
www.eastsidekingaustin.com

twitter @eastsidekingatx
daily 7p - 1:45a
dinner. late night
$ cash only. first come, first served

Yes. Please: *bruxelles biere , curry bun, fried brussels sprout salad, beet home fries, thai chicken karaage, ginger garlic jasmine rice, pro qui's buns*

I guess this is as good a place as any in the book to talk in depth about food trailers in Austin. The history of this culture began... oh blah blah blah. There are a zillion different spots you can read about the whole food cart thing, and everybody is falling over themselves to explain it. But instead of reading about it, just start experiencing it, i.e., get thee out to eat. And **East Side King** is a good starting spot. Get lubed first at **Liberty Bar,** which is the "host" building in front, and then order a round of owner/chef Paul Qui's Asian-inspired, vegetarian friendly fare. Doesn't this sound like a good way to end your day?

east side showroom

sally bowles would dine here

1100 East Sixth Street
Corner of Medina (East Austin) *map E12*
512.467.4280
www.eastsideshowroom.com

twitter @east_showroom
daily 5p - 2a (kitchen closes
sun - wed 11p thu - sat midnight)
dinner. late night
$$ reservations accepted for parties of
six or more

Yes, Please: *rum daisy, the diablo, the showroom, antelope tartare, gulf shrimp & curried grits, quail & preserved oranges, lamb ribs with fried okra*

When you walk into East Side Showroom and your eyes adjust from the bright Texas sun to the darkness of the room, you half expect to see a lineup of saucily attired, red-lipped, raven-haired bordello girls attending to languidly lounging customers. Owner Mickie Spencer has created a bawdy world here that's not only a hoot to hang out in but one that makes you wish you weren't wearing jeans and flip flops. As you dig into chef Sonya Cote's delicious locally-sourced fare with a cleverly composed drink in hand, forgive yourself for your modern grubbiness and embrace the romance of the **East Side Showroom**.

franklin barbecue

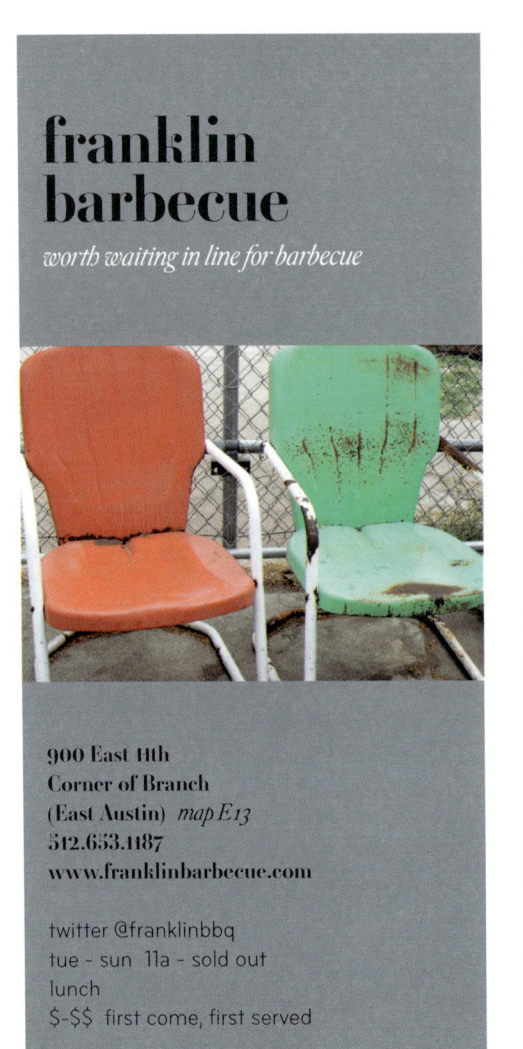

worth waiting in line for barbecue

900 East 11th
Corner of Branch
(East Austin) *map E13*
512.653.1187
www.franklinbarbecue.com

twitter @franklinbbq
tue - sun 11a - sold out
lunch
$-$$ first come, first served

Yes, Please: *cold big red, sweet leaf tea, pulled pork sandwich, tipsy texan sandwich, two meat plate, any of the meats by the pound*

There are not a lot of things I would stand in line in searing heat for. But for a good plate of barbecue, I would take the sunburn and armpit outpour. Which is exactly what I did to eat lunch at **Franklin Barbecue**. They open at 11am, but the line forms about 10 minutes before. And you'd best get here before noon, because this meaty goodness sells out fast. Grab your order, a cold Big Red, sit down, and feel the eyes of the hungry line dwellers upon you. You could gloat as you're devouring the melt-in-your-mouth brisket. But don't, because soon enough you'll be back in that line.

helm

beautifully crafted, handmade men's shoes

4704 A East Cesar Chavez
Near Springdale (East Austin) *map S08*
512.609.8150
www.helmhandmade.com

twitter @helmhandmade
by appointment only
online ordering. custom orders / design

Yes, Please: *helm styles > brock, emi, poppy, ray ray raleigh denim, samuel, tante, dunkel, timmy bob*

Joshua Bingaman is a multi-tasking master. When I first met him he had just opened **Progress Coffee**, which is at the forefront of eco- and socio-concious coffee houses. Then he decided it was time to get into roasting, which begat **Owl Tree Roasting**. Somewhere in his downtime he began **Helm**, a handmade shoe concern. How does one man do it all? In Joshua's case, he's got a great team behind him that includes the Turkish craftsmen who cobble these new-style-with-an-oldfangled-twist shoes. A pair will immediately identify you as someone who wears their individuality proudly.

justine's brasserie

a bit o' france in east austin

4710 East Fifth Street
Near Spencer Lane (East Austin) *map E14*
512.385.2900
www.justines1937.com

mon, wed - sun 6p - 2a
dinner. late night
$$-$$$ reservations recommended

Yes, Please: *l'enfant terrible, muscat de frontignan, escargots a la bourguignonne, aspèrges blanches with sabayon sauce, steak tartare, confit de canard*

A restaurant without buzz is like a dog without a bark. Yes, there's the serene appeal that comes with silence, but after a while you want some sound. Suffice to say, **Justine's Brasserie** is not the basenji of the Austin eating scene, but more like a French bulldog. It's got tons of energy in somewhat of a compact package and it's cute in a toughy type of way. People flow in here from all over town and the energy that comes with the mix is intoxicating. Or maybe the intoxication comes from the drinks that the bar is pouring. Whatever it is, **Justine's** has got the buzz.

owl tree roasting
local roaster with a big heart

Retail: 500 San Marcos Street at Progress Coffee
Corner of 5th (East Austin) *map E15*
512.493.0963
www.owltreeroasting.com
www.progresscoffee.com

twitter @owltreeroasting
mon - fri 6:30a - 7p sat 7:30a - 7p
sun 7:30a - 5p
$ first come, first served

Yes, Please: *blends > progress house, mexican chiapas, jo's, mohawk, bird's barbershop brew, wally 10, beef & pie beefy's after beer espresso*

It's hard for me to grasp how certain things work. For example, how is it when I talk into a tiny little box, somebody answers their tiny little box and they can hear my voice? And how is it that by roasting a bitter little bean, something as delicious as a cup of hot coffee can be made? Both are mysteries to me, but the multi-talented Joshua and his partners at **Owl Tree Roasting** can at least answer the coffee question. Here they roast small batches of carefully sourced beans to create coffee not only for their own label but also for businesses around Austin, like **Bird's Barbershop**. Now this I understand.

switched on

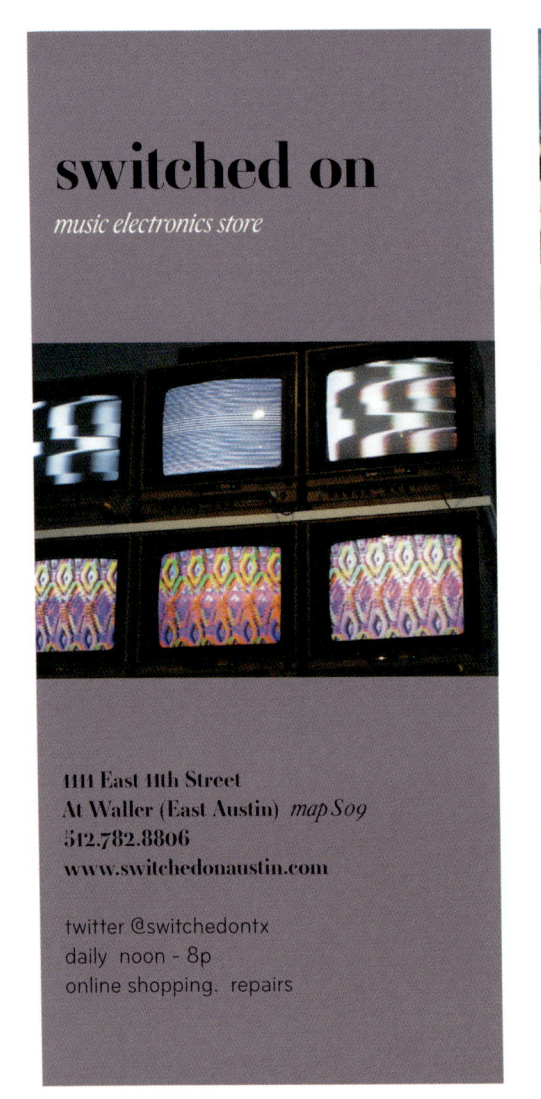

music electronics store

1111 East 11th Street
At Waller (East Austin) *map S09*
512.782.8806
www.switchedonaustin.com

twitter @switchedontx
daily noon - 8p
online shopping. repairs

Yes, Please: *rhodes mark one stage piano, wurlitzer mlm (music learning machine), estey m101 travel organ, bleep labs thinaomagoops*

You've got to imagine that a girl who played in a synth pop band called Matisse Video in the mid '80s is going to have a jones for a vintage synthesizer store, which is why the tractor beam of synth sounds pulled me to **Switched On**. Not only are there primo vintage Moogs and Casios here, there are also brand new thingamajigs like the cool Thingamagoop. Though I'm the furthest thing from a tech geek, this place makes me want to spend hours (days even) fiddling about making crazy sounds and wonky beats.

rather.com 61

trailer space records

ts loves rock n' roll

1401-A Rosewood Avenue
Corner of Angelina (East Austin) *map S10*
512.524.1445
www.trailerspacerecords.com

tue - sat noon - 10p
sun - mon noon - 6p
live music

Yes, Please: *lps by > bad sports, the golden boys, pygmy lush, the big dirty, wild america, nature boys, mind spiders*

When I was in high school and college it didn't occur to me to hang out at a record store. Not sure why; maybe it was because the local pizza place had cuter guys. Maybe if **Trailer Space Records** existed back in my day, I would have hung out here. I'm sure there are not only some cute guys that work here, but more importantly there's great music to be bought and live music to listen to when bands play on the stage that's in the midst of the store. Yeah, I think I can wrap my head around this hanging at the record store thing, and you should too.

yellow jacket social club

charmingly ramshackle east side saloon

1704 East 5th Street
Between Comal and Chicon
(East Austin) *map E16*
512.480.9572
www.yellowjacketsocialclub.com

daily 11a - 2a
brunch. lunch. dinner
$-$$ first come, first served

Yes, Please: *marinated pork loin satay, piloncillo chz, roasted beets, chevre and arugula sandwich, cuban beef sandwich*

The buzz about this divey-hip watering hole near the railroad tracks traveled fast. Soon after the owners of the **Yellow Jacket Social Club** set up shop in beloved east side institution **Café Mundi's** charmingly ramshackle saloon and patio space, Austin's café cognoscenti descended for afternoon cocktails and updated bar snacks. Worship at the bar crafted from timbers reclaimed from an old church, and thank the patron saint of hipsters for the abundant and affordable plates of Mediterranean and Cuban-influenced café food. Along with the cool cocktails and beer on tap, the wifi flows freely—your laptop and your dog are equally welcome, and there's no jacket required.

midtown

ut / the drag

eat

e17 texas french bread

shop

- **s11** bell and bird
- **s12** catbird paper
- **s13** complete clothing
- **s14** dog and pony
- **s15** fiddler's green music shop
- **s16** nice kicks
- **s17** rootin' ridge toymakers

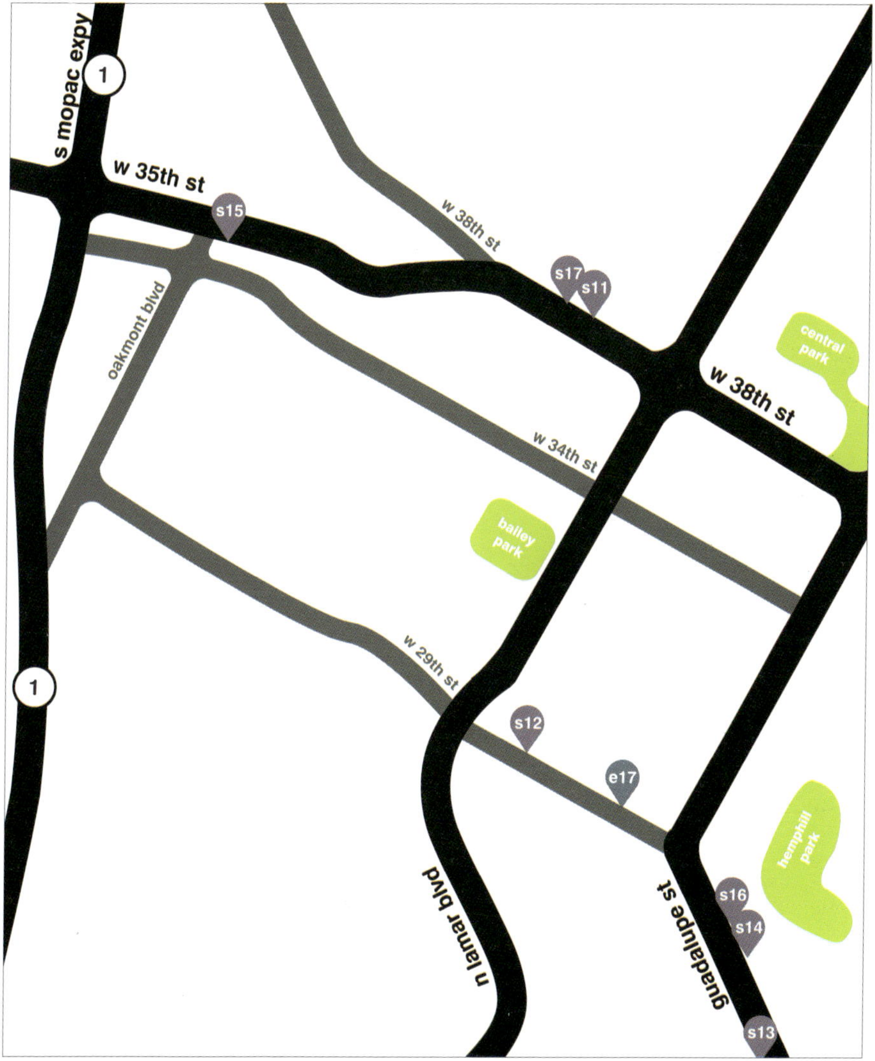
s mopac expy
1
w 35th st
s15
w 38th st
s17
s11
oakmont blvd
central park
w 38th st
w 34th st
bailey park
1
w 29th st
s12
e17
hemphill park
n lamar blvd
guadalupe st
s16
s14
s13

bell and bird

exquisite custom and antique jewelry

1206 West 38th Street #1102
Near Lamar in the 26 Doors Plaza
(Midtown) *map S11*
512.407.8206
www.bellandbird.com

tue - fri 11a - 5p sat 11a - 3p
or by appointment
custom design / orders

Yes. Please: *antique > tiara ring, 14k wedding bangle, aquamarine earrings, opal diamond topaz ring, cut steel chandelier earrings*

When I'm working on these books, I fantasize that I will discover a place that leaves me speechless. Bell and Bird fulfilled this dream. Pause for a moment of silent awe. What has me verklempt about B & B are the timeless, sublime pieces of antique jewelry that the lovely couple Rhianna and Cyrus have gathered from far and wide. Much of the jewelry here is from the century before the last century, which means when you buy one of these pieces you'll become part of the long storyline and journey that your newfound heirloom treasure has been on.

catbird paper

pretty papers

900 West 29th Street
Corner of Pearl (Midtown) *map S12*
512.436.8506
www.catbirdpaper.com

twitter @catbirdpaper
mon - sat 10a - 4p
custom design / orders

Yes. Please: *catbird press invitations, announcements & correspondence, snow+graham, elum, cavallini, roost, gianna rose atelier, hello lucky*

During the working day I type, text and twitter, and I've noticed over the last couple of years my handwriting has begun to suffer due to my reliance on electronics. My once beautiful, sloping script has become an ugly, jagged scrawl. So the prescription I've given myself is to start writing more notes and letters. The perfect place to find proper accoutrements is **Catbird Paper**. This slightly off the beaten path spot has a perfectly pretty selection of all things paper, including their own line of goods. Goodbye texts, hello letters!

complete clothing

streetwear joint

1904 Guadalupe Street
Corner of Martin Luther King Jr.
(Midtown) *map S13*
512.473.8244
www.complete-clothing.com

twitter @complete_z
mon - thu noon - 7p fri - sat noon - 8p
sun 1 - 5p
special orders

Yes. Please: *stussy, undefeated, huff sf, primitive, benny gold, clae, the hundreds, g-shock*

While working on this book, I got stuck on one of the UT side streets during a massive run-a-thon. As I sat idling away, I noticed how many of the runners were wearing UT emblazoned outfits, which is obviously *de rigueur* if you attend. Friends, I want you to know there's a whole world of clothing out there for you that's not burnt orange and it can be found at **Complete Clothing**, right in your 'hood. Zaul Zamora has pulled together a great selection of both clothing and sneakers that will make you look fresh without making you look ghetto. Shopping here shows you're learning something.

dog and pony

spunky mix of women's clothing

2712 Guadalupe Street
Between West 27th & Hemphill Park
(Midtown) *map S14*
512.236.8777
www.dogandpony.us

tues - sat noon - 7p sun noon - 5p
online shopping

Yes, Please: *uzi printed pillow, osborn booties, vintage cutoffs, georgia varidakis rabbit necklace, john cho moore calfskin wallet*

College fashionistas must have been stoked when Dog and Pony popped up in their 'hood. Although there are copious shopping options near the UT campus, most of the retail stores are watered down national chains selling factory-made personality. **Dog and Pony** brings some Lower East Side street energy, a drop of vintage, and some edgy footwear to the Guadalupe strip. Even those of us who are (ahem) a bit past our college years can find handmade or handpicked goods that comprise the backbone to a look: well-cut prints by Dusen Dusen and Uzi, idiosyncratic jewelry by Georgia Varidakis, or embroidered Osborn Oxfords. Old dog, meet new tricks.

fiddler's green music shop

a strummer's wonderland

1809 West 35th Street
Between Mo-Pac and Jefferson
(Midtown) *map S15*
512.452.3900
www.fiddlersgreenmusicshop.com

tue - thu 10a - 8p fri - sat 10a - 6p
sun noon - 5p
online shopping. classes. lessons.
repairs. jams

Yes, Please: *collings mandolins, ellis mandolins, resonator ukeleles, ohana ukeleles, vega banjos, vintage gibson banjo, dusty strings harps*

Ever since I heard the riff at the end of Rod Stewart's song "Maggie May," I have loved the sound of the mandolin. For half my life I have been telling myself I must learn how to play one, though I figure it might be smart to learn how to play a guitar first, which I'm still working on. Walking around **Fiddler's Green Music Shop** lit the mandolin fire inside me again, as this is a mandolin wonderland. Here you can find instruments for beginners or professionals, some handcrafted, and a whole raft of other stringed instruments. Coming here makes me itch to start a-strumming as well.

nice kicks

sneaker freaker heaven

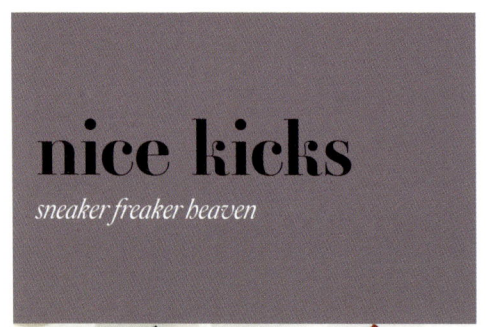

2815 Guadalupe Street
Between 28th and 29th
(Midtown) *map S16*
512.320.8100
www.nicekicks.com

twitter @nicekicksshop
mon - sat 11a - 8p sun noon - 6p
online shopping

Yes, Please: *nike air max 90 "infrared," converse auckland racer, nike air max 95 "grape," the supra avenger, nike air mariah*

When it comes to footwear, I'm somebody who talks the language of No. 6 clogs or Rachel Comey wedges, meaning I couldn't begin to tell you what's of the moment in conjunction to sneakers. That's why I'm sending you to **Nice Kicks**, because Matt Halfhill knows everything I don't know and more. Heck, he's got so many zillions of people reading his blog, he could put together his own **Nice Kicks** army of sneaker freakers, many of whom show up at this über-cool store the moment a limited edition shoe hits the shelves. Watch out, though, I might be the first in line.

rootin' ridge toymakers

hand crafted wooden toys

1206 West 38th Street #1105
Near Lamar in the 26 Doors Plaza
(Midtown) *map S17*
512.453.2604
www.rootinridge.com

mon - fri 10a - 5p   sat 10a - 4p
custom orders / design

Yes. Please: *rootin' ridge wooden toys > push rattle, timbali, texas native animals puzzle, texas aggravation puzzle, wheeled animals, bird feeder*

If your three year old asks you to buy her a Squinkies Gumball Surprise and you can't bear another piece of plastic in your house, there's a fantastic alternative: a handcrafted wooden toy from **Rootin' Ridge Toymakers**. Though plastic toys are everywhere we look, chances are they aren't going to be heirlooms, but instead a part of our ever-growing landfills. Paul Kyle at **Rootin' Ridge** makes toys that your child will play with and love now, but that will be something they can give to their children thirty years from now. These are the types of toys that make childhood special.

rather.com

texas french bread

beloved austin bakery-turned-restaurant

2900 Rio Grande Street
Corner of 29th (Midtown) *map E17*
512.499.0544
www.texasfrenchbread.com

twitter @txfrenchbread
mon - sat 7a - 10p sun 8a - 6p
breakfast. lunch. dinner. bakery
$-$$ reservations recommended

Yes, Please: *alice's french toast, house granola & white mountain yogurt, la niçoise on focaccia, tagiatelle & seafood puttanesca, black drum with oven roasted potatoes*

If you think I'm going to talk about bread here, you're wrong. Yes, **Texas French Bread** is a bakery and has long been an Austin institution helmed by Judy Wilcott. But then her sons Murph and Ben decided that it was time to give **TFB** a twist, and they began hosting dinners. And when I say dinners, I don't mean something slopped on toast. The Wilcott boys serve beautiful food that has foodies citywide a-twitter (both literally and figuratively). My meal here was delicious, but I will admit I spent a good deal of my evening with my eyes glued to the dessert case. This is a bakery, after all.

midtown

hyde park

eat

e18 antonelli's cheese shop
e19 casey's new orleans snowballs
e20 foreign & domestic

shop

s18 breakaway records

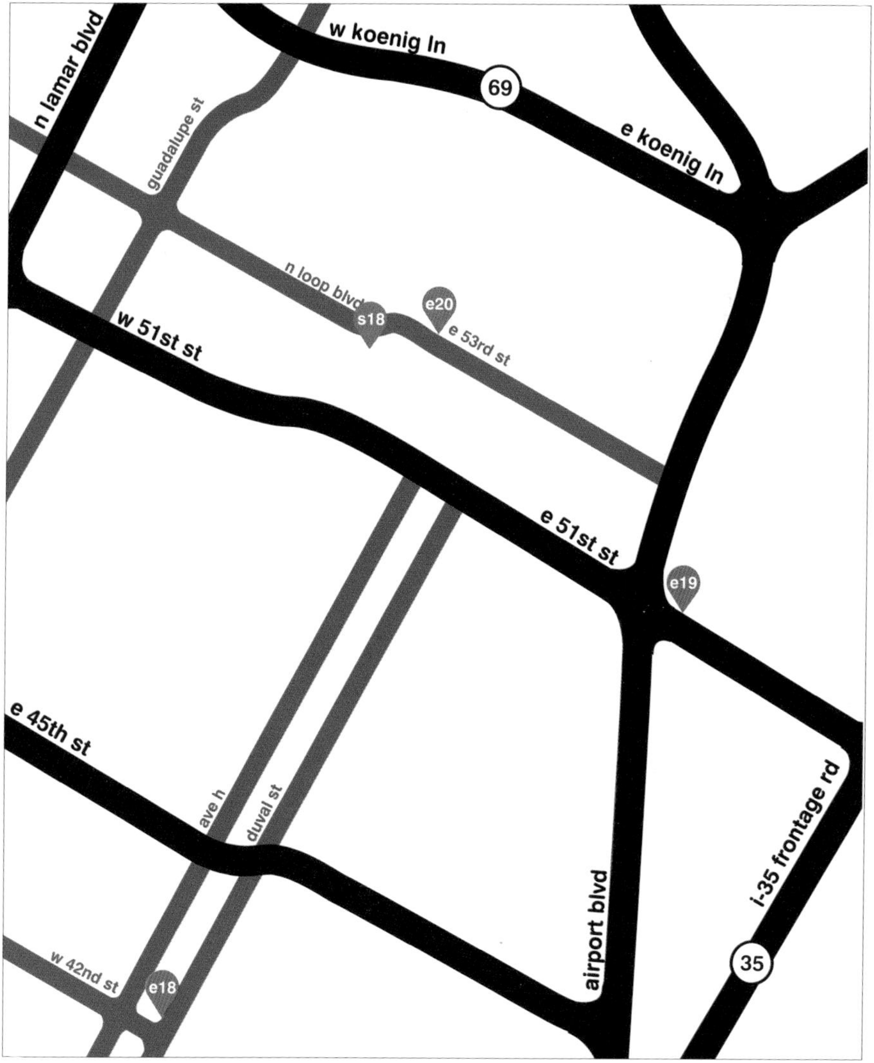
n lamar blvd
w koenig ln
69
e koenig ln
guadalupe st
n loop blvd
s18
e20
e 53rd st
w 51st st
e 51st st
e19
e 45th st
ave h
duval st
airport blvd
i-35 frontage rd
35
w 42nd st
e18

antonelli's cheese shop

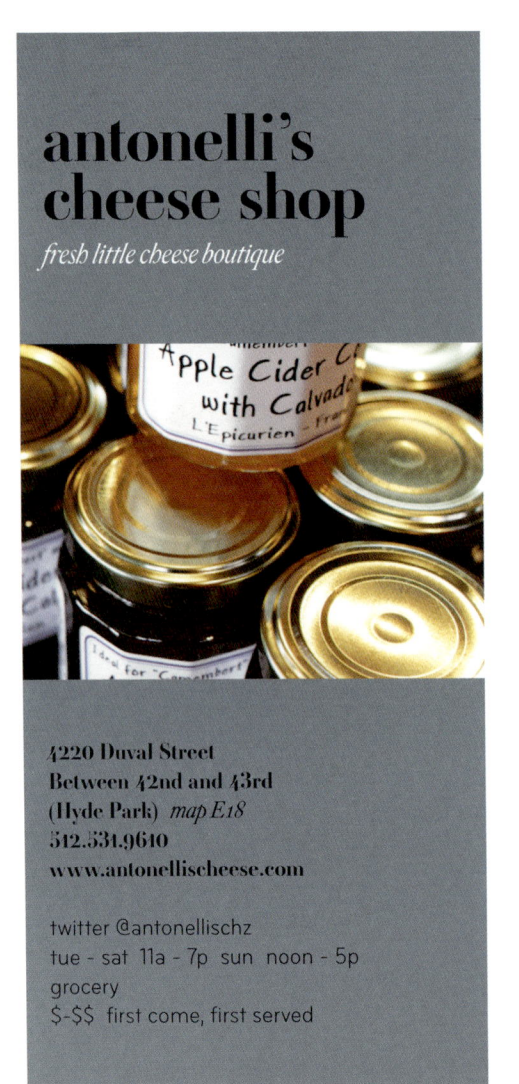

fresh little cheese boutique

4220 Duval Street
Between 42nd and 43rd
(Hyde Park) *map E18*
512.531.9610
www.antonellischeese.com

twitter @antonellischz
tue - sat 11a - 7p sun noon - 5p
grocery
$-$$ first come, first served

Yes, Please: *'06 chateau du bloy bergerac,
ckc farms midnight chevre, ardrahan farmhouse cheese,
veldhuizen texas star cheddar*

Taleggio, Red Hawk, Epoisses }...

Tomme Crayeuse, Morbier, Colby }...

Cheddar, Manchego, Tarentaise }...

Parmigiano-Reggiano, Vella Dry Jack, Midnight Moon }...

Rogue River Blue, Roquefort, Gorgonzola }...

velvety, lanolin

water buffalo

wet hay, tangy

Lactose Intolerant

amount of lactose   high

There's a scene in the movie French Kiss where Meg Ryan's character has a transformative experience with cheese. After years of lactose intolerance-induced terror, a train ride through Provence and a smarmy yet charming Frenchman break down her fromage barriers. If you suffer from a cheese phobia, I suggest a visit to the charming (with absolutely no smarm) **Antonelli's Cheese Shop**. Within minutes the knowledgeable staff will have you eating out of their hands and you will find yourself besotted with even the stinkiest of cheeses.

milk   cheeses

rather.com

breakaway records

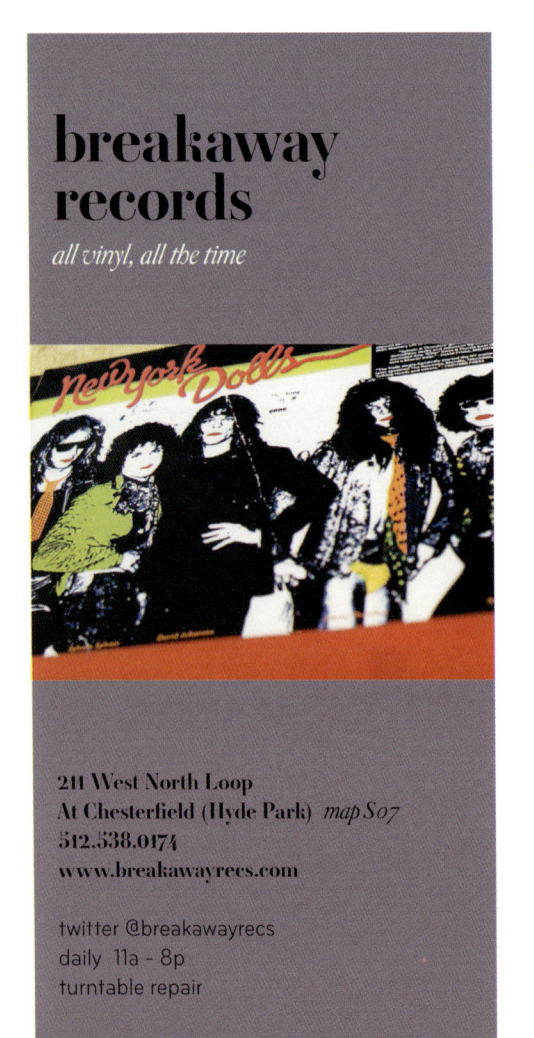

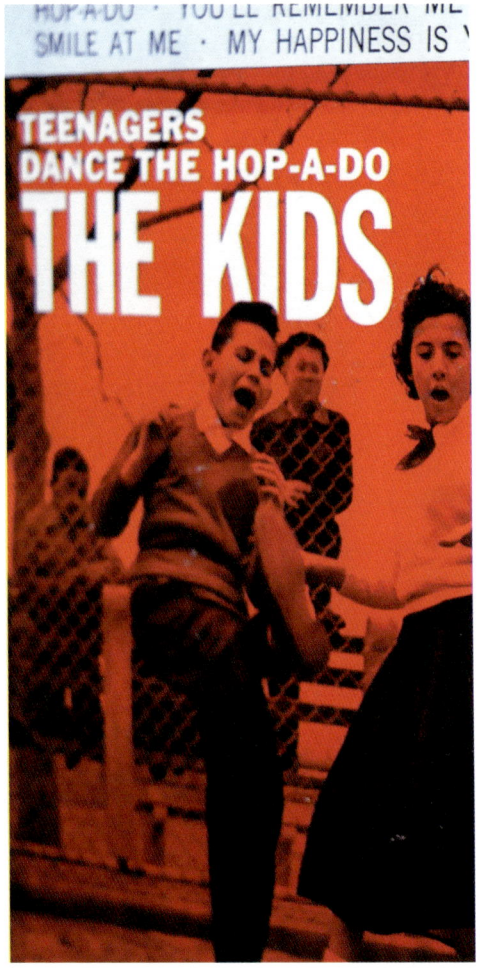

all vinyl, all the time

211 West North Loop
At Chesterfield (Hyde Park) *map S07*
512.538.0174
www.breakawayrecs.com

twitter @breakawayrecs
daily 11a - 8p
turntable repair

Yes. Please: *sterling 45 receiver, gino washington "out of this world," units "new way to move," tangerine dream "stratosfear"*

I don't have a turntable because I gave it away along with my Captain & Tennille and Henry Gross records. But now I need a turntable again. I'm tired of the soul-less quality of CDs and MP3s. I want to hear the buzz and scratchiness of a needle skimming along vinyl; I want to hear the yowling of Joey Ramone or Screamin' Jay Hawkins the old school way. And so I'll go to **Breakaway Records** and buy myself a vintage turntable, and while I'm at it I'll stock up on vinyl, both new and old. Then I'll lock myself in a room just like I'm 15 again and listen to music until my head spins happily.

casey's new orleans snowballs

icy cold goodness

808 East 51st Street
Corner of Airport (North Austin) *map E19*

open daily from noon (apr - sep)
treats
$ cash only. first come, first served

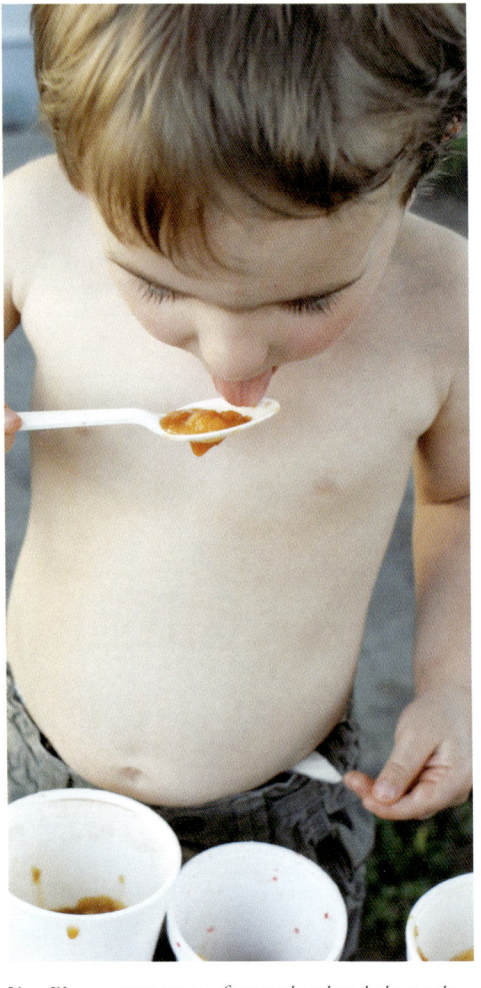

Yes. Please: *snowcones > famous chocolate, leche canela, dreamsicle, orchid cream vanilla, banana fudgesicle, hurricane, pink grapefruit*

Sno-cones. Shaved ice. Water ice. Snowballs. I could explain the differences between these icy delights, but that's a waste of time because they are all #1: cold, #2: sweet, and #3: delicious. If you're going to spend any time in this town during the warmer months—of which there are many—you're going to develop a meaningful relationship with at least one of these cooling treats. My latest fave is **Casey's New Orleans Snowballs**. They make a chocolate snowball (created with homemade chocolate sauce) that will rock your 95 degree world. Though the stand is a bit out of the way, don't let that stop you from a visit.

foreign & domestic

inventive culinary creations

306 East 53rd Street
Between Avenue H and Avenue G
(Midtown : Hyde Park) *map E20*
512.459.1010
www.fndaustin.com

twitter @foreigndomestic
tue - thu 5:30 - 9:30p fri - sat 5:30 - 10p
sun 10a - 2p
brunch. dinner
$$-$$$ first come, first served

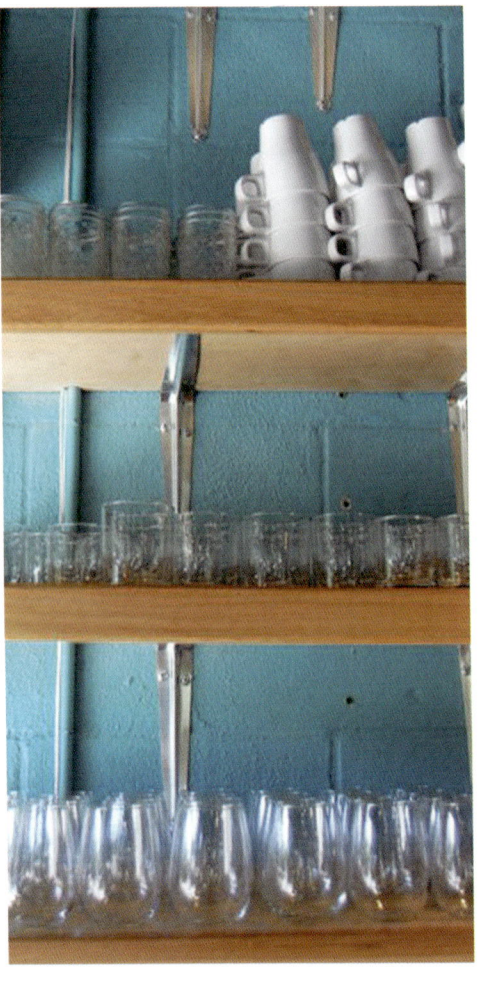

Yes, Please: *grilled & whipped lardo, crispy beef tongue, crab lasagna, almond tart with lemon ice and whipped crème fraiche*

I admit that I am not a fan of the gratuitous use of offal. In the wrong hands, the nose-to-tail movement can lead to less-than-pleasant dinners of nasty little bits that feel more biology lab than haute cuisine. Chef Ned Elliott's hands are talented in the extreme, however, and at **Foreign & Domestic**, I find myself slurping up lardo, crispy tongue and beef heart tartare. For a restaurant that prides itself on the use of the whole animal, F & D is a surprisingly friendly place for vegetarians. Read: priest strangler pasta with tomato fondue and truffle butter. A dinner of this caliber certainly qualifies one for dessert—don't miss pastry chef Jodi Elliott's insanely good seasonal creations.

north austin

eat

- e21 apna bazaar
- e22 chen's noodle house
- e23 chosun galbi
- e24 el caribe
- e25 little deli
- e26 musashino sushi dokoro
- e27 panaderia chuy
- e28 sambet's cajun deli & firey foods store
- e29 tâm deli & cafe

shop

- s19 austin bike farm
- s20 gene rogers optical
- s21 mod green pod
- s22 spruce upholstery
- s23 the corner shoppe mall
- s24 tiny's western shop
- s25 uptown modern

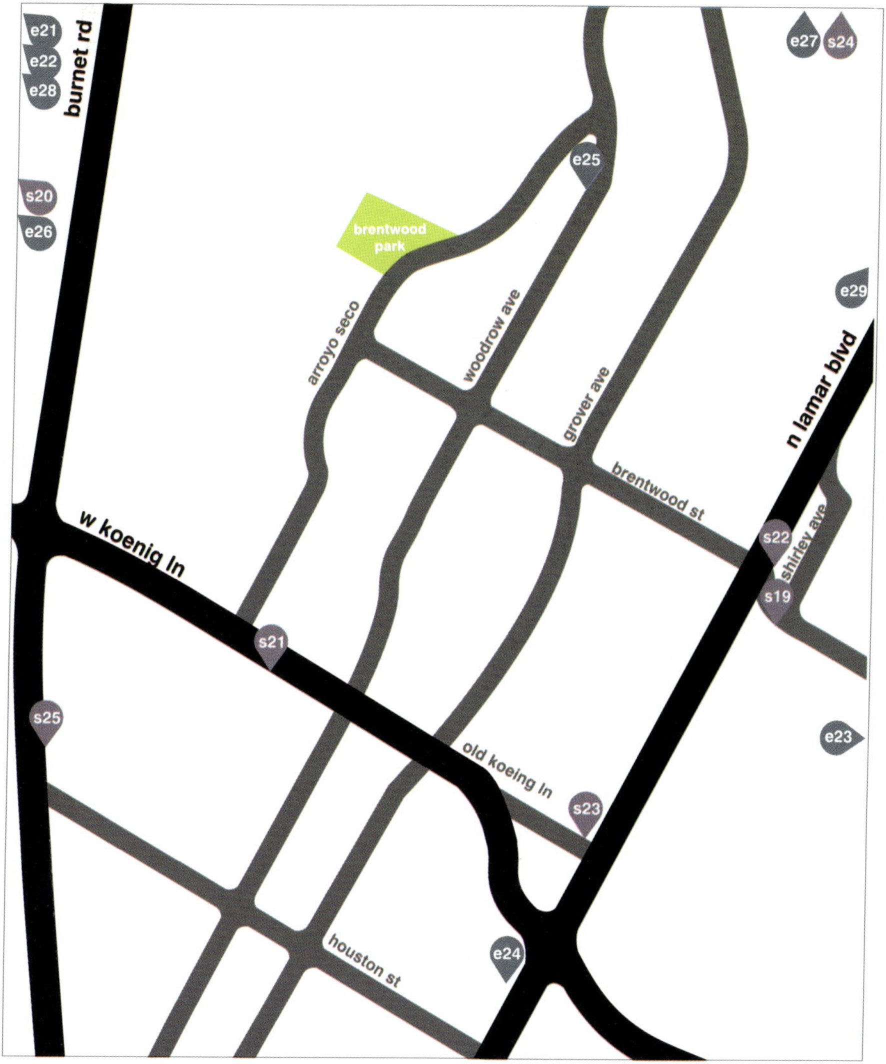

e21
e22
e28
burnet rd
e27
s24
e25
s20
e26
brentwood park
e29
arroyo seco
woodrow ave
grover ave
n lamar blvd
brentwood st
w koenig ln
s22
shirley ave
s19
s21
s25
e23
old koeing ln
s23
houston st
e24

apna bazaar

indian, pakistani and bangladeshi grocery store

8650 Spicewood Springs Road #133B
At 183 Frontage (North Austin) *map E21*
512.249.0202
www.apnabazaaraustin.com

mon - sat 11a - 9p sun noon - 9p
grocery
$-$$

Yes, Please: *tetley ginger tea, swad almond oil, gopi paneer mdh masalas, golden temple durum atta flour, great selection of spices, beans & rices, fresh fruits & veg*

It's a particular quirk of mine, when I'm traveling in foreign lands, that before I head to any monument, temple or museum I aim for the local markets—both the open air markets and the more modern, westernized groceries. I guess then it makes sense here in the States that I'm always sniffing around for great ethnic groceries, and **Apna Bazaar** falls firmly into that category with its mix of Indian, Pakistani and Bangladeshi goods. Even if you don't cook any of these cuisines, this small market is a treasure trove of spices and rices and ingredients that can be used in your everyday diet.

austin bike farm

new bikes, old bikes

6516 Shirley Avenue
Just Off Lamar (North Austin) *map S19*
512.419.1911 / 512.585.0127 (emergencies)
www.austinbikefarm.com

tue - sat 11a - 7p
trade-ins. repairs

Yes, Please: *new bikes > linus, commençal, blkmrkt, 183rd street, civia, vintage bikes, parts & more parts*

I can't tell you how many days in a row I drove north on Lamar to see if **Brazos Trading Company** was open, its pile of old Schwinns and well worn Levi's tempting me through the dusty window. One day, in a fit of frustration after finding it closed again, I drove around the corner and there was a sign for **Austin Bike Farm**. A sign from the bike gods? I followed it and came upon where old bikes not only come to die but also come back to life when people buy their parts. Add on new bikes for sale, bike repair and trade-ins. Yes, the bike gods are happy.

chen's noodle house

divine hand-cut noodles

8650 Spicewood Springs Road
At 183 Frontage (North Austin) *map E22*
512.336.8888

mon, wed - sun 11a - 9p
lunch. dinner
$ cash only. first come, first served

Yes. Please: *hot tea, leek pie, green onion pancakes, lamb noodle soup, noodle with egg & tomato, steamed dumplings, lamb skewer*

Something about this town makes me want to explore its every nook and cranny, including the plethora of ethnic eateries that populate the Northern outskirts. **Chen's Noodle House**, in the same strip mall as **Apna Bazaar** and **Sambet's Cajun Deli**, is a gem that deserves a bit of a road trip. Where do I begin my love letter? This is a stamp-sized spot with all of four tables and a succinct menu of eight items. What inspires rhapsody are the soups brimming with Zhao's hand-cut noodles, which, in their imperfection, are pretty damn perfect.

rather.com

chosun galbi

korean barbeque and more

713 East Huntland Drive
Near I35 Frontage (North Austin) *map E23*
512.419.1400
www.chosungalbiaustin.com

daily 10a - 10p
breakfast. lunch. dinner
$$ reservations accepted

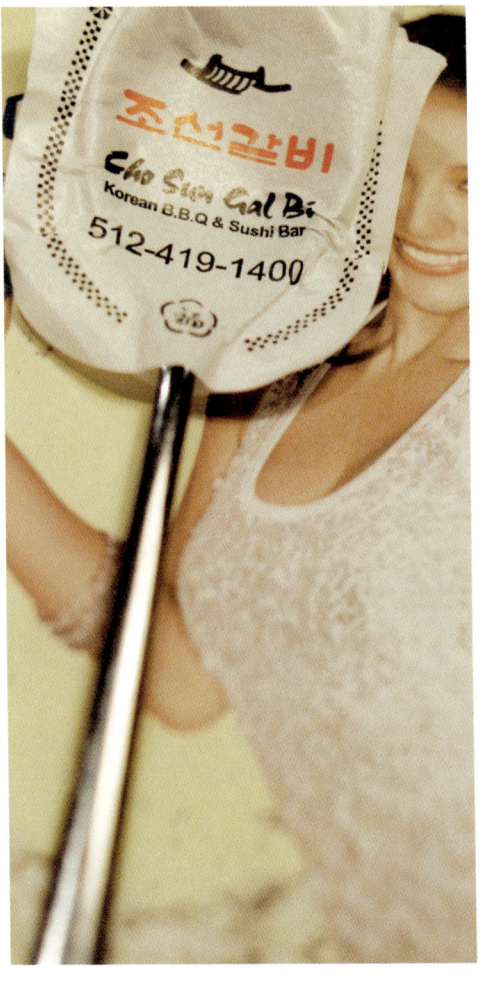

Yes, Please: *bite beer, bok bunja soju, dwe ji bulgogi (spicy marinated pork bbq), gam ja tang (pork back bone stew), goon mahn doo (dumplings), bibimbob*

Chosun Galbi is a continuation of the story I began telling at Chen's. At the tail end of a day spent circling the outskirts of Austin, I was exhausted from eating, so I figured I would revive myself by eating more at **Chosun Galbi**. There was some solid reasoning behind this, as Korean cuisine is known for its restorative qualities. Maybe it's the omnipresent red pepper in Korean cooking, but as soon as I dove into a bowl of spicy crab meat soup, I found new reserves of energy. Or at least enough oomph to get myself to the car and aim towards a cushy sofa with my name on it.

el caribe

salsalicious interior mexican restaurant

5610 North Lamar Boulevard
Near Koenig Lane (North Austin) *map E24*
512.452.6207

mon - thu 11a - 9p fri 11a - 10p
sat 10a - 10p sun 10a - 9p
breakfast. lunch. dinner
$-$$ first come, first served

Yes, Please: *house margarita, strawberry licuados, queso caribeño, tortilla soup, steak à la mexicana, huachinango al mojo de ajo, mojarra frita, sopapillas*

Because a portion of my life is dedicated to a quest for good queso, there's always a place in this book where I must focus on my beloved hot fromage melange. **El Caribe** has good queso. In fact, if I didn't have to share my queso with my cohorts and fellow judges Joe and Marianne, I would have hoovered the entire bowl here like a gluttonous melted cheese loving pig. I resisted the urge and instead focused on the visually uninspiring but tastefully inspired salsa bar. **El Caribe** might be a hole-in-the-wall, but the food is really darn good.

gene rogers optical

vintage and new eyewear

2700 W. Anderson Lane #404
At Northcross Drive
(North Austin) *map S20*
512.451.7316

mon - fri 9a - 5:30p sat 10a - 3p
online shopping

Yes, Please: *vintage > lozza over-sized circular frames, thick black cat eyed frame. new > shuron clear freeway frames, lacoste sport aviator sunglasses*

Tucked away in a North Austin strip mall between a Thai restaurant and a sports bar is a secret that eyewear aficionados have guarded for many years. Gene Rogers' father opened his first storefront in 1954 and then expanded the franchise to four locations. When the family business consolidated in the '70s to this one location, Gene and his wife scored the mother lode of deadstock vintage frames—with styles spanning three decades. Cat-eye, check. Gigantic granny specs that hipster girls covet, yes. Cherry-red, 1960s Italian frames that belong in a Fellini film, sigh. Welcome to spectacle heaven.

little deli

a classic east coast pizzeria and much more

7101-A Woodrow Avenue
Between Piedmont and St. Johns
(North Austin) *map E25*
512.467.7402
www.littledeliandpizza.com

twitter @littledeli
mon - sat 11a - 9p
lunch. dinner
$-$$ first come, first served

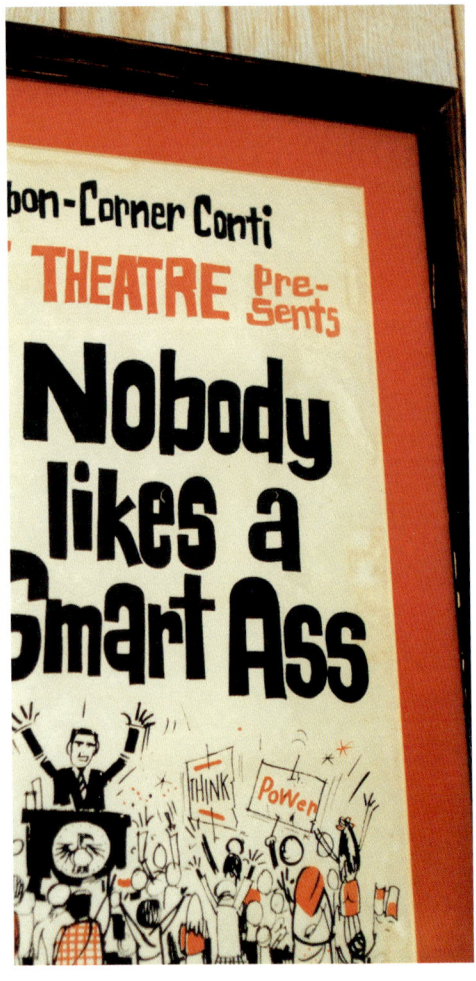

Yes, Please: *orange crush, new jersey style pizzas > pepperoni, rollatini, white; italian wedge sub, meatball sub, italian cream cake*

As a native West Coaster who lived in NYC for a number of years, I found myself confused by the description of the pizza at **Little Deli** as "Jersey Shore style." Not so pretty images of Snooki and The Situation filled my head, but then I tasted the pizza and all I could think of was how darn good it was. Still befuddled by the difference between New Jersey and New York pizzas, I asked **Little Deli** owner Tony Villani to explain. He noted that both styles belong under the banner of East Coast style, which is derived from Neapolitan: thin-crust pizza. A-ha! Mystery solved. Now I can focus on eating. I'll take a sub to go with my pizza, please.

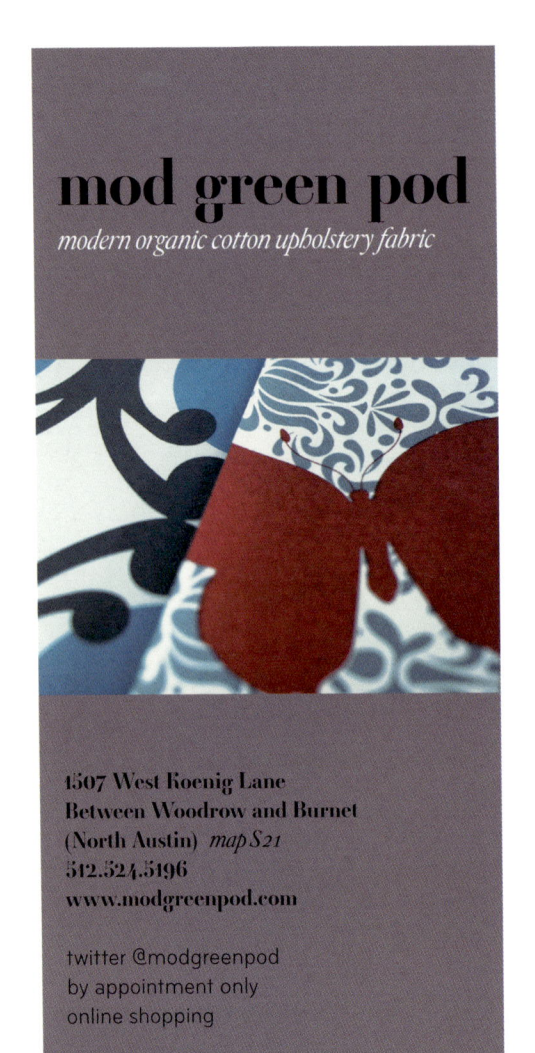

mod green pod
modern organic cotton upholstery fabric

1507 West Roenig Lane
Between Woodrow and Burnet
(North Austin) *map S21*
512.524.5196
www.modgreenpod.com

twitter @modgreenpod
by appointment only
online shopping

Yes, Please: *fabrics > bloom, grand jubilee, glimmer; wallpapers > delight, butterfly jubilee, tote bags*

Even before the now defunct Domino Magazine reawakened the wallpaper desire in me, I was dreaming about having walls that went beyond satin, eggshell or gloss as a decorative element. So it's a bit sad that I still don't have a stitch of wallpaper hung. I'm hoping **Mod Green Pod** might be the place that gets me off my behind. These patterns are so compelling, so contemporary, so graphically fresh that it makes me want to wallpaper the whole house, inside and out. And while I'm at it I might cover the cars, the pets and anything else that I can use **MGP's** fabrics on. I feel a transformation coming.

musashino sushi dokoro

tokyo style sushi

**3407 Greystone Drive
(Under Chinatown Restaurant)
At Southbound Mo-Pac Expwy Access
(West Austin)** *map E26*
**512.795.8593
www.musashinosushi.com**

twitter @musashinosushi
see website for hours
lunch. dinner
$$-$$$ reservations accepted for parties of seven or more

Yes, Please: *choya plum wine, takashimizu house sake, sawagani (deep fried mini crabs), avocado kama, shokado bento, omakase, tempura ice cream*

Though I know some people find joy in eating a cream cheese b.l.t. sushi roll, I'm not one of them. I guess I'm a bit of a food purist at heart. When it comes to Japanese fare I like to search out places that feature Japanese food, not westernized Japanese food. **Musashino** is exactly what I'm talking about. Smokey, the owner/chef, is legendary in town not only for his food but also for his incredible knife skills. I suggest sitting at the sushi bar so you can watch the food prep choreography behind the counter. It's mesmerizing, and the results are delectable.

panaderia chuy
enticing mexican bakery and more

8716 Research Boulevard #290
At Ohlen (North Austin) *map E27*
512.374.9910

daily 6a - 10p
bakery. deli
$-$$ first come, first served

Yes. Please: *bolillos, conos rellenos de crema, mantecadas, bombines, besos de fresca, banderillas, ice cream, breakfast tacos & tortas*

Mexican bakeries, panaderias, appeal to me. So much so that I find myself going out of my way so I can buy galleta de grajellas (oatmeal cookies with sprinkles) or pan de huevo (sugared egg bread). Sadly, though, when I get home and dig into my treasures, they generally never taste as good as they look. Then I found **Panaderia Chuy**. Madre de Dios! There's a veritable cornucopia of baked goods here and they all taste as good as they look, and **Chuy's** breads may well be some of the best in town. Going out of my way has never tasted this good.

sambet's cajun deli & firey foods store

where to get your cajun on

8650 Spicewood Springs Road #111
At 183 Frontage (North Austin) *map E28*
512.258.6410
www.sambets.com

mon - thu 11a - 8p fri - sat 11a - 9p
lunch. dinner
$-$$ first come, first served

LAISSEZ LES BON TEMP ROULEZ

Yes, Please: *sweet tea, muffaletta, po' boys, crawfish etouffee, deep-fried turkeys, fresh live crawfish, alligator meat, hundreds of hot sauces*

I think this place has the longest name of any of the businesses featured in this book: Sambet's Cajun Deli & Firey Foods Store. The time it takes you to say this is about the same amount of time it would take you to realize that your taste buds were burning from one of the hot sauces they sell. Even if this place wasn't in my favorite food strip mall in Austin (see **Apna Bazaar** and **Chen's Noodle House**), I'd still go out of my way to eat their savory Cajun delights and spend an hour trying to figure out which of the zillions of hot sauces to take home with me.

spruce
furniture redesign studio

6607 North Lamar
Corner of Brentwood
(North Austin) *map S22*
512.454.8181
www.spruceaustin.com

twitter @sprucehome
mon - fri 10a - 6p sat noon - 4p
online shopping (etsy). classes.
custom orders / design

Yes, Please: *the beatnik barry white sofa, cupid chairs, willie pillows, the care bear chair, cherry clossom chairs, rising tide settee, flames of passion headboard*

I want you to know that even though I'm sure I'd like you, you are not welcome to come to my house. I know this sounds rude, but I would be too embarrassed to have you see my ratty couch that has been gnawed on by a long succession of stinky dogs. I would invite you to come to my house, though, if I got my disintegrating couch reupholstered at **Spruce**. Or, even better, I should throw the couch out and get a new couch, chairs and lamps here. Whether it's new upholstery you need or a funky throw pillow or a piece of furniture, the ladies here will have you covered. Sorry for the pun.

tâm deli & cafe

go-to spot for authentic vietnamese

8222 North Lamar #D33
Between Powell and Meadowlark
(North Austin) *map E29*
512.834.6458

mon, wed - sun 10a - 8p
breakfast. lunch. dinner
$-$$ first come, first served

Yes, Please: *fresh kumquat lemonade, jicama spring roll, shrimp & shredded yam crispy fritters, vietnamese crepe, garlic butter shrimp banh mi, banh choux*

There are Pointer sisters, Andrew sisters and, unfortunately, Hilton sisters, but none can hold a candle to the sisters behind the delicious Vietnamese food at **Tâm Deli & Cafe**. Though not all of the sisters are involved at **Tâm** on a daily basis, the feeling of family is pervasive and the cooking reflects it. For example, the kumquat lemonade is made with the fruit that comes from one of the sisters' kumquat trees. What I wouldn't give to get an invite to one of their family meals. Oh, wait... coming here is probably just as good.

the corner shoppe mall

a trove o' taxidermy

5900 North Lamar Boulevard
At Old Koenig Lane
(North Austin) *map S23*
512.451.7633
www.taxidermyking.com

twitter @taxidermyking
mon - sat 9a - 6p
online shopping. appraisals

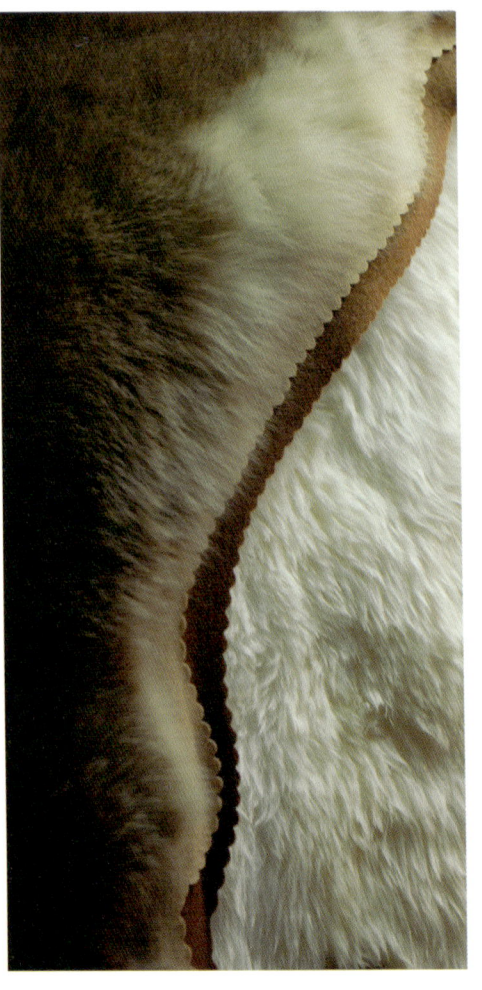

Yes, Please: *taxidermy > bears, exotic deer, pheasant, warthog, water buffalo, horns; mexican blankets*

Animal lovers, please hear me out. I am an animal lover too, and I don't relish the idea of shooting and then stuffing Gentle Ben. But I do have a soft spot for taxidermy, especially in the context of visiting **Deyrolle**, the legendary natural history shop in Paris. Even though **The Corner Shoppe Mall** is on a nondescript corner of Lamar instead of the Left Bank, it has a pretty magnificent collection of taxidermy, some of which might work with the décor of my house. Okay, maybe not the hyena, but the squirrel driving a toy car could be a good conversation piece.

tiny's western shop

mexican rodeo and western wear shop

8403 Research Boulevard
Between Fairfield and Clearfield
(North Austin) *map S24*
512.476.1277

mon - sat 11a - 8p sun noon - 6p
custom orders / embroidery

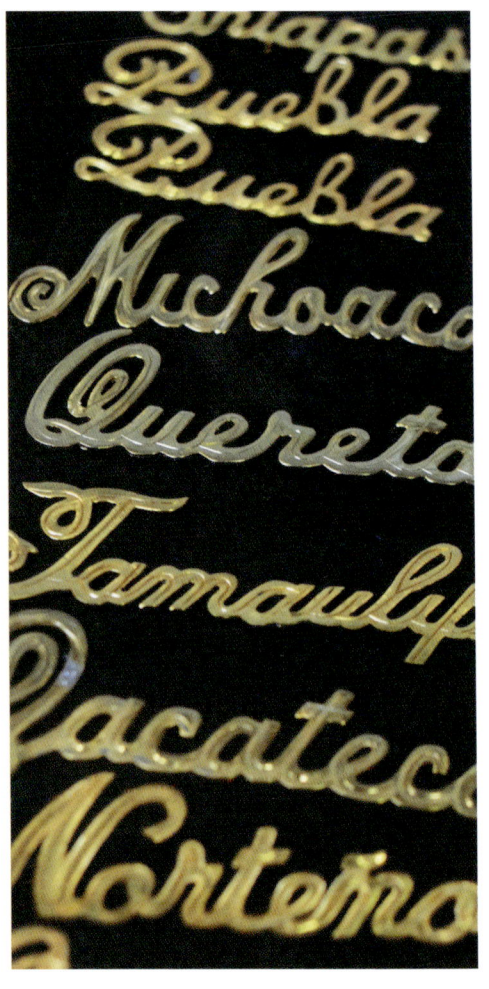

Yes, Please: *clothing > mestizos, resistol rodeo gear, wrangler pro rodeo competition gear, rocky mountain jeans; dos de oro boots & cowboy hats, cowboy hat pins*

I have never been to a charreada (a traditional Mexican rodeo), and last I looked at my busy calendar, I don't have plans to go to one. But that won't stop me from going to **Tiny's Western Shop**. It's chock full of gear that one might wear if they were competing in or going to a rodeo, or, if they are like me, just love western wear. There's a wealth of goodness to be found here, from white leather moccasins to little kids' guayaberas to customizable pins you can attach to your cowboy hat (or whatever you like). **Tiny's** is pretty mighty in my esteem.

uptown modern

great vintage finds

5453 Burnet Road
Near West Koenig Lane
(North Austin) *map S25*
512.452.4200
www.uptownmodernaustin.com

mon - sat 11a - 6p sun noon - 5p
wish lists

Yes, Please: *'70s tufted leather couch, '50s hans wegner folding chair, '60s gem locke leather chairs, '60s west german floor vase, '60s salterini bench*

My entire adult life I have lived in older houses that often have had a fair amount of hand-me-down furnishings. Because of this I have a fantasy of someday building a modern, low-slung house. Something that would use lots of wood, stone, a fair amount of concrete, and modern furniture. Even though my vision is modern, I know that to give this fantasy dwelling soul I will mix in vintage furniture, and **Uptown Modern** would be the perfect spot to shop. Jean Heath carries a wide selection of mid-century pieces including outdoor furniture and vintage clothing to boot. Fantasy house, here I come.

south austin

eat

e30 barley swine
e31 el meson taqueria
e32 gourdough's
e33 home slice pizza
e34 hotel san josé lounge
e35 la boîte
e36 lulu b's
e37 odd duck farm to trailer
e38 olivia
e39 perla's seafood & oyster bar
e40 uchi/uchiko
e41 whip in

shop

s26 bows + arrows
s27 feathers
s28 ga ga
s29 howl interiors
s30 laced with romance
s31 moss
s32 roadhouse rags
s33 schatzelein
s34 spartan
s35 stag
s36 stitch lab
s37 w3ll people

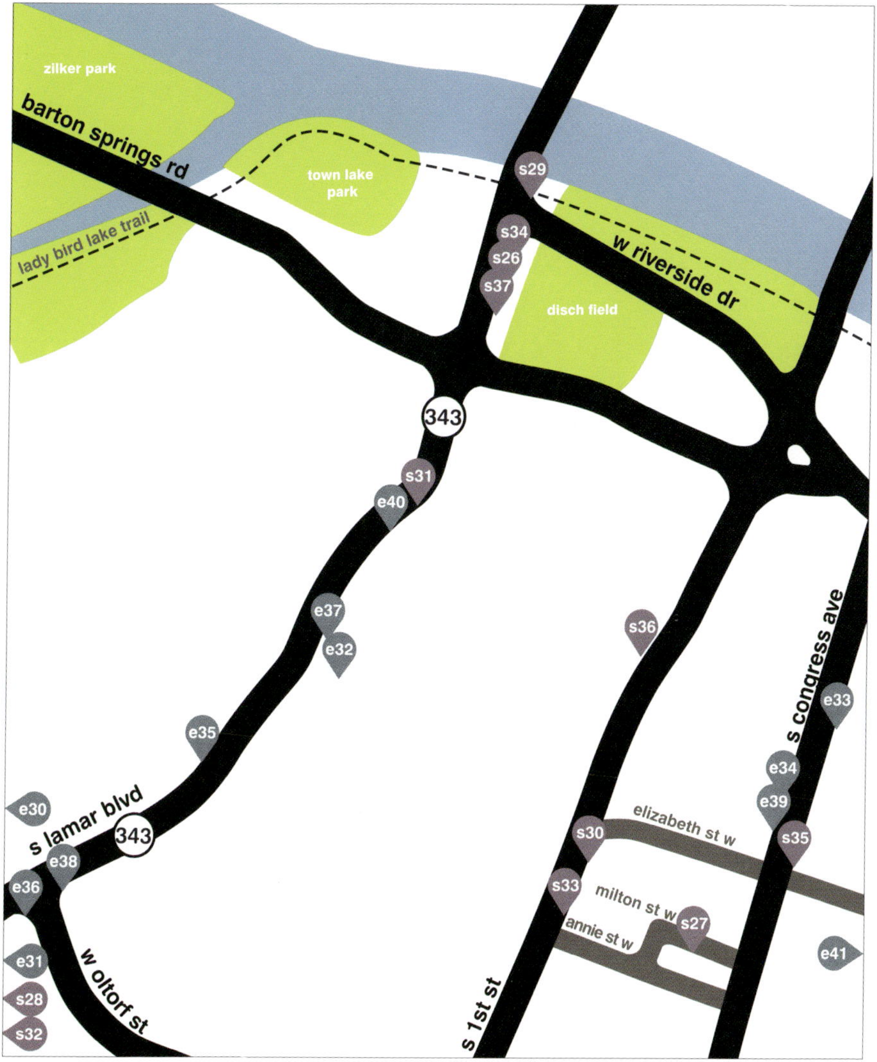

zilker park
barton springs rd
town lake park
lady bird lake trail
w riverside dr
disch field
343
s29
s34
s26
s37
s31
e40
e37
e32
s36
e35
e33
s congress ave
e34
e39
e30
s lamar blvd
343
e38
e36
s30
elizabeth st w
s35
s33
milton st w
s27
annie st w
e41
e31
s28
s32
w oltorf st
s 1st st

barley swine

a celebration of pork and beer

2024 South Lamar Boulevard
Between Oltorf and Hether
(South Austin) *map E30*
512.394.8150
www.barleyswine.com

twitter @barleyswine
mon - fri 6 - 11p sat 5 - 11p
dinner
$$-$$$ reservations recommended

Yes, Please: *grilled rabbit terrine with bacon-liver mousse, scallop with grilled pork belly and shishito pepper, smoked pecan fudge with cocoa nibs and salted caramel ice cream*

On Saturday nights, I like to go to Barley Swine to dine with friends I haven't met yet. The communal tables at this quietly amazing gastropub encourage conversation and connection over small plates of deceptively simple and rustic flavors. *Food & Wine* Best New Chef 2011 Bryce Gilmore cultivates close relationships with local farmers and ranchers. His dishes are inspired by the season and the menu changes every few weeks. Diners are encouraged to order three dishes per person, and "substitutions are politely declined." Believe me, I'll never be one to say, "Hold the pork belly" or "Easy on the brown butter." Small space, small plates, huge flavor.

bows + arrows

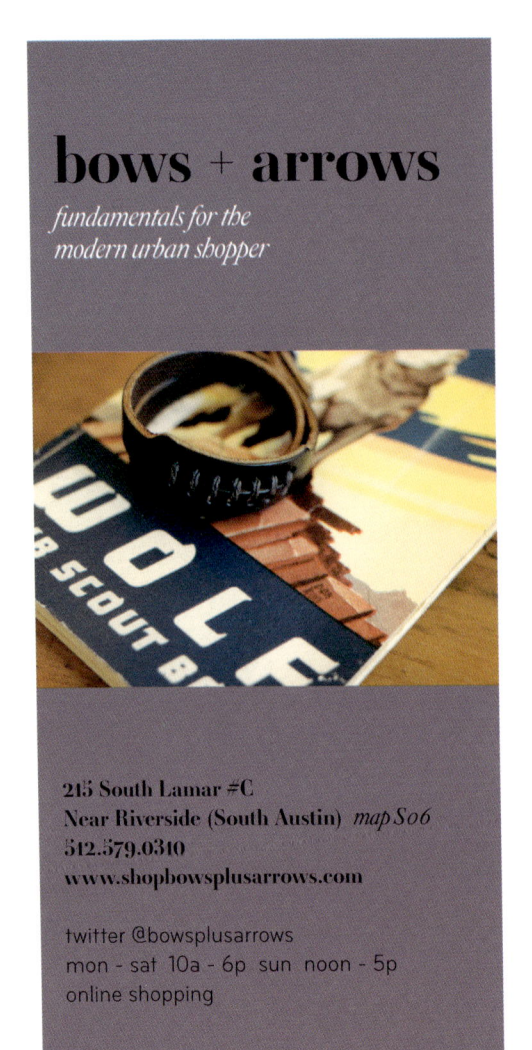

*fundamentals for the
modern urban shopper*

215 South Lamar #C
Near Riverside (South Austin) *map S06*
512.579.0310
www.shopbowsplusarrows.com

twitter @bowsplusarrows
mon - sat 10a - 6p sun noon - 5p
online shopping

Yes, Please: *steven alan, shipley & halmos, karen walker, apc, band of outsiders, manu by lauren manoogian, n.d.c. boots, portland general store*

There are many a modern terms that are overused, but the one that grates on me the most is BFF. It's just so Paris and Nicole that I want to scream. It's not that I'm opposed to good friends; take for example the side-by-side businesses **Bows + Arrows** and **Spartan**. This is friendship at its finest. B + A is the clothing part of this alliance, and owner Lauren Wilkins gives as much attention to women's clothing as to men's, focusing on fashion forward lines that are known for their classic simplicity. Based off all the things I want here, I'm thinking Lauren and I might be future BFFs, if I can force myself to say it.

el meson taqueria

a little out of the way, but oh so worth it

5808 Burleson Road
Between Montopolis and Judson
2038 South Lamar Boulevard
Near Oltorf (South East Austin) *map E31*
512.416.0749

mon - fri 6:30a - 2:30p sat 7a - 2p
breakfast. lunch
$ cash only. first come, first served

Yes, Please: *pineapple barrilitos, chorimigas, huevos motulenos, egg & cactus breakfast taco, tinga, calabacitas, enchiladas, chilorio*

Some people go on vision quests; I go on meal quests. El Meson Taqueria is a perfect example of my willingness to go on a trek for deliciousness, as it's pretty much between nowhere and nowhere. But despite its location, El Meson is definitely a somewhere because it's so darn good. The menu is small, the tortillas are a revelation of freshness, and the flavors are perfection. If you aren't willing to go to great lengths like I am, though, the kind El Meson folks have just opened another location closer in on the South side.

feathers

desirable women's vintage clothing

1700B South Congress Street
Enter on Milton (South Austin) *map S14*
512.912.9779
feathersboutiquevintage.blogspot.com

twitter @feathersvintage
daily 11a - 7p

Yes. Please: *jody california, shopping with anthony, gunne sax, geoffrey beene; shoes > halston, a. gomez, yves st. laurent*

It takes a fair amount of panache to pull off wearing vintage clothing, and what I mean by that is nobody wants to look like Carol Brady sporting a '70s pantsuit or like Donna Summer in one of her less fortunate '80s era disco get-ups. The way to make vintage look modern is to not mimic the past but to take bits and pieces of it and incorporate it into your style. **Feathers** is the perfect place to get some lady fabulous pieces, whether it's a pair of YSL stilettos or a Bill Gibb's mink halter top. Throw your new purchases on with a skinny pair of jeans and kapow, you're super-stylin'.

ga ga
if only i were a little kid again

2810 Manchaca Road
Corner of Lamar (South Austin) *map S16*
512.462.4510
www.gagababygaga.com

mon - sat 10a - 7p sun noon - 6p
registries

Yes, Please: *decaf plush, axel & hudson, knuckleheads, stella industries, cardboard designs teepee, dwell studio bedding, plan toys drumset*

Even though the word gaga has been co-opted by an outré, Saran Wrap-wearing pop star, I still associate the term with the cooing sound of babies. It's what I'm assuming Caroline Hernandez was thinking when she named her charming new children's store **Ga Ga**. Though I am of the belief that it's a parental right to dress your kids in cute clothing, I get a little scared when adults gussy up their tykes in styles that make them look like they should be at Studio 54. You won't find those get ups here; instead you'll find fun, modern clothes that celebrate childhood.

rather.com **139**

gourdough's
big. fat. donuts.

1219 South Lamar Boulevard
Across From Lamar Square Drive
(South Austin) *map E32*
www.gourdoughs.com

twitter @gourdough
see website for hours
treats
$ cash only. first come, first served

Yes, Please: *dublin dr. pepper, donuts > mother clucker, flying pig, miss shortcake, naughty & nice, blue balls, the puddin'*

Some things that weigh as much as one of Gourdough's donuts: a newborn baby, a bowling ball, or 120 Hostess mini-donuts. I might be exaggerating a touch, but these suckas are huge. Am I complaining? Hell no! It's just more donut to love, and you can buy one to feed your whole family. Again, just joking, because it's not too taxing to down one on your own. Don't think that you are going to have one for breakfast, though, as the rest of your day might be spent in repose. Knowing this, the trailer opens at 5pm, just in time for desert after eating at **Odd Duck** next door.

home slice pizza

neighborhood pizza joint with hand-tossed pies

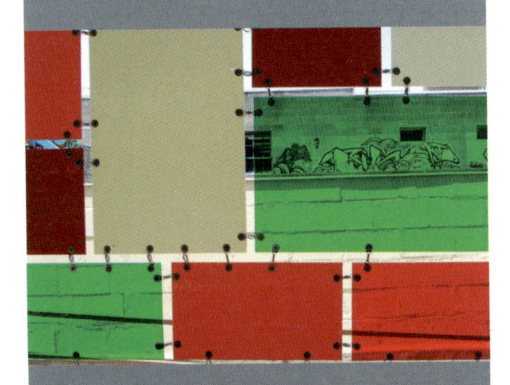

1415 South Congress Avenue
Between Elizabeth and Gibson
(South Austin) *map E33*
512.444.7437
www.homeslicepizza.com

twitter @homeslicepizza
mon, wed - thur 11a - 11p
fri - sat 11a - midnight sun noon - 11p
lunch. dinner
$-$$ first come, first served

Yes, Please: *real ale fireman's #4, pear gorgonzola salad, antipasto, white pie with spinach, white clam pizza, margherita pizza, homemade cannoli*

Since 2005 the crew at Home Slice has been satisfying Austin's taste for thin-crusted New York style pie. A night at **Home Slice** is always a party—funky, vintage pizza parlor décor is the perfect atmosphere in which to enjoy a sausage, ricotta cheese and roasted red pepper pie with a pitcher of locally brewed beer and a side of cranked-up, just-right '70s jukebox ballads. If you're on the move, grab a slice from **More Home Slice** next door, but we never mind the wait on the patio out back, which affords fabulous hipster-watching opportunities while sipping a Liberace-prosecco and Izze blackberry soda with a little twist of lemon.

hotel san josé lounge

a favorite place for a drink in austin. still.

1316 South Congress
Between James And Gibson
(South Austin) *map E34*
512.444.7322
www.sanjosehotel.com

twitter @sanjosehotel
mon - thu 5p - midnight
fri - sun 3p - midnight
beer / wine. snacks
$-$$ first come, first served

Yes, Please: *shandy, real ale rio blanco pale ale, tinto de verano, champassion, wine sangria, tamari roasted almonds, house marinated olives*

I feel like I'm having a long-term affair with the Hotel San José Lounge. I want to come here looking foxy, because this place is so remarkably good-looking. And then once I'm here and I'm feeling the intensity of the attraction, I morph into full lust looking at the simple yet desirable drink and snack menu. Will the sexy, fruit-ridden sangria make me weak at the knees or will the champassion tempt me to throw myself into the pool, à la Anita Eckberg in *La Dolce Vita*? Whatever the draw is, I know that I will keep on coming back again and again and again.

rather.com

howl interiors

furniture and curios for the urban bohemian

705A South Lamar Street
Between Juliet and Bluff
(South Austin) *map S19*
512.291.2123
www.howlinteriors.com

twitter @howl_interiors
tue - sat 11a - 6p   mon or by appointment
online shopping

Yes. Please: *coquillage, turkey jesus, neptune cocktail table, leo in a box, coke bottle collage, custom farmhouse tables, grotto revival etagere, neo-brutalist mirrored console*

Barry, the mad genius behind Howl Interiors, had my full attention after uttering just two words: Grotto Revival. Brilliance! I've got nothing against Mid-Century Modern or Shaker, but enough already. I've been searching for that special creative someone who uses the techniques of shock and awe, which is certainly Barry's modus operandi. The Grotto style he's riffing off of goes back to 18th century Italy, when classical furniture was embellished in a rococo style with natural elements. Barry's modern day approach might take the form of an octopus cocktail table or a winged Jesus. Now I'm shocked and awed.

la boîte cafe

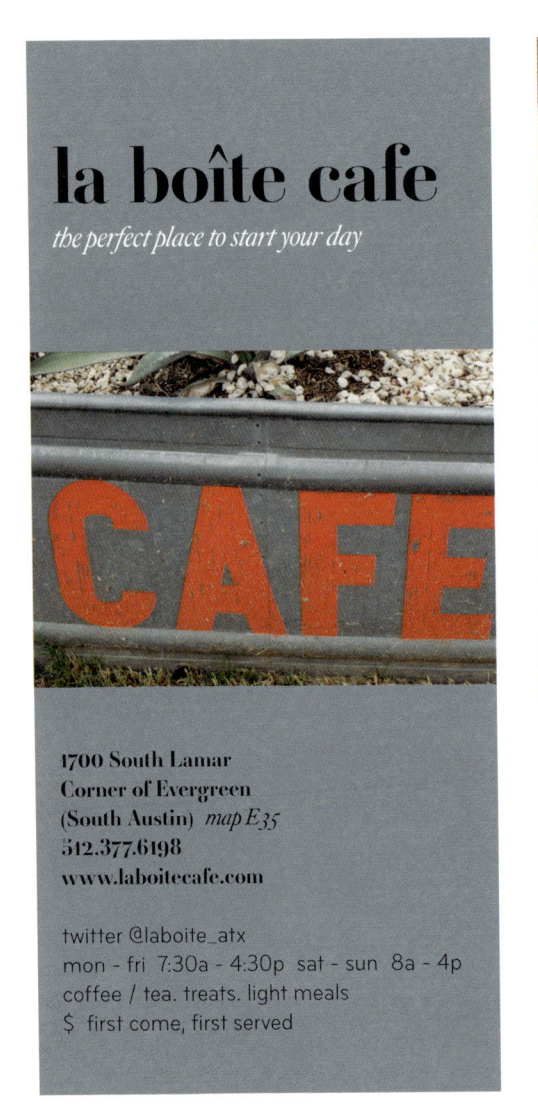

the perfect place to start your day

1700 South Lamar
Corner of Evergreen
(South Austin) *map E35*
512.377.6198
www.laboitecafe.com

twitter @laboite_atx
mon - fri 7:30a - 4:30p sat - sun 8a - 4p
coffee / tea. treats. light meals
$ first come, first served

Yes. Please: *espresso, french press coffee, iced coffee toddy, almond croissant, pain au chocolat, sausage brioche, macarons, ham, gruyere & mustard sandwich*

> ✸ Sandwich du jour ✸
> ✸ Pederson Farms All Natural
> DaiQue Fireman's Farm Mustard &
> Gruyere Cheese

Ahhhhh, La Boîte, I have such a crush on you. There are certain places that radiate good vibes, and this shipping container/coffee spot/café has it in spades. Maybe it's the way it sits perched on a small hill fronting a strip mall, or the sails that stretch out as awnings. These are nice touches, but really it's the good coffee, delish pastries (some from the best baker in Austin, Barrie Cullinan) and light savories that look good, taste good and are just downright good. It all comes together to make **La Boîte** a place that deserves your affection.

laced with romance

rock n' roll playground

1601 South 1st Street
Corner of Monroe (South Austin) *map S30*
512.576.9693
www.lacedwithromance.com

mon - sat 11a - 7p sun noon - 5p
online shopping

Yes, Please: *frye 1970's black label lace-up boots, rima hyena giantic crystal ring, dust & drag fringe leather bag, vintage springsteen tour t-shirt, hand-dyed silk camisoles*

Living in a city where there's a drum kit in every basement, I've always hoped some rocker cool would rub off on my wardrobe—to no avail. Enter **Laced with Romance**. The moment my eyes saw Stephanie Fellabaum's beautifully edited racks of vintage and cabinets of gothic jewels, my inner Joan Jett urged me toward slouchy biker boots, skintight denim, and burned-out concert tees. My Anita Pallenberg side was satisfied by the flowing silks, oversized coats, and floppy hats. A silver rattlesnake ring here, a wispy tunic there, and suddenly I've got backstage cred. Put another dime in the jukebox, baby.

lulu b's

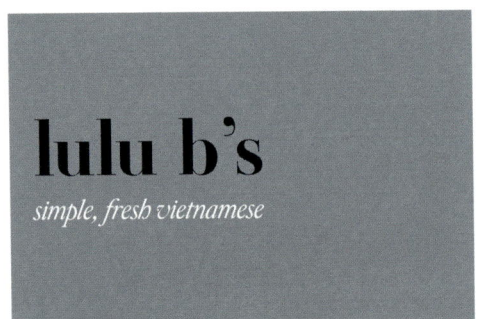

simple, fresh vietnamese

2113 South Lamar Boulevard
Near Oltorf (South Austin) *map E36*
512.921.4828
www.myspace.com/lulubssandwiches

twitter @lulub0107
tue - fri 11a - 4p sat 11a - 5p
lunch. early dinner
$ cash only. first come, first served

Yes. Please: *vietnamese coffee, chrysanthemum tea, green bubble tea, banh mi > lemongrass chicken, chinese bbq pork; vermicelli bowls, salad rolls*

Recently, the cult of banh mi, the classic Vietnamese sandwich, has moved into the mainstream. I'm loving that I can find these mouth-watering sandwiches more handily now, but I'm bothered by some of the places that are using foodstuffs like peanut butter or American cheese as ingredients. Hello! Really? If you want a modernized version of this sandwich but don't want the culinary lunacy, head to **Lulu B's** truck. Here they are building banh mi that very much mimic the classics but are lighter and fresher. The same light touch is applied to the other Vietnamese fare here, too, and that spells y-u-m.

rather.com 153

moss

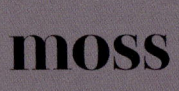

refined consignment

**705b South Lamar Boulevard
Between Bluff and Juliet
(South Austin)** *map S31*
512.916.9961
www.mossaustin.com

mon - thu 11a - 7p   fri - sat 11a - 8p
sun noon - 6p
accepts consignments

Yes. Please: *derek lam silk blazer, fiona paxton beaded necklace, chanel tweed bolero, gucci strappy studded booties, common thread tangerine camisole*

The ritual of dressing for an evening out is an endangered pleasure in this mad, rushed world. It should start with a bubble bath, a cocktail, jazz on the turntable, red lipstick, perfume, and slipping into your frock with proper anticipation for the night. **Moss** has resurrected that old-school energy by gathering a chiseled set of designer clothes, bags and shoes. The space is elegant and spare. The skilled staff and the lean, high-caliber collection will inspire you to linger and enjoy. Best of all, everything from the Chanel boleros to the Gucci stilettos is consigned, so you'll have change left in your clutch for that night out.

odd duck farm to trailer

where fine dining and food cart culture converge

1219 South Lamar Boulevard
Across From Lamas Square Drive
(South Austin) *map E37*
512.695.6922
www.oddduckfarmtotrailer.com

tue - sat 5:30 - 10p
dinner
$-$$ cash only. first come, first served

Yes, Please: *ciabatta toast with beets, arugula & goat feta; brussels sprouts with capers & mortadella, soft boiled duck egg, grilled asparagus, goat ricotta & toast*

There's the saying, "so and so is a bit of an odd duck," and there's cold duck, which is cheap bubbly. Then there's **Odd Duck Farm to Trailer**, which is neither strange nor liquid but a fabulous eating experience. Bryce has mixed fine dining with food cartism and come up with a tasty formula. This may well be the only place where a dish like grilled rabbit loin and goat ricotta is served in a paper boat more accustomed to holding greasy nachos. Sitting at the tables here on a warm night with music playing and kids munching their monster **Gourdough's** donuts seems like Austin in a lovely nutshell.

olivia

fine dining with panache

2043 South Lamar Boulevard
Near Oltorf (South Austin) *map E38*
512.804.2700
www.olivia-austin.com

twitter @olivia_78704
see website for hours
brunch. dinner
$$-$$$ reservations recommended

Yes. Please: *porta rocha white port cocktail, seductively described wine list, chef's tasting menu, grilled escargot skewer & garlic parsley butter*

When people planning to visit Austin ask me about the restaurant scene here, their questions usually focus on barbeque, food carts and barbeque. Very rarely do they inquire about the fine dining options, which is a mistake, because they'd miss out on a gem like **Olivia**. This is the type of f.d. establishment that I heart: a pretty room that's inviting and stylish, a wait staff that's knowledgeable and highly professional (too often missing in modern restaurants), and last but most important, chef James Holmes' beautifully crafted menu tastes dee-vine. **Olivia** gives fine dining a good name.

perla's seafood & oyster bar

a little bit of new england in texas

1400 South Congress Avenue
Corner of Gibson (South Austin) *map E39*
512.291.7300
www.perlasaustin.com

see website for hours
brunch. lunch. dinner
$$-$$$ reservations accepted

Yes, Please: *the parasol, (512) wit beer, half dozen half shell oysters > sheepscott (maine), totten inlet (washington); ahi tuna tartare with quail egg, steamed wreckfish*

I eat copious amounts of food when I'm working on these books, and most of it (though sadly not all of it) is really good. On occasion one dish will rise above all others to become the dish I will dream about until I'm 100 (though if I keep eating this way I won't make it that long). For this book, the title goes to **Perla's** lobster stock, cheddar and green onion grits. If my husband and child hadn't been with me I would have devoured the whole thing and licked the dish until my tongue was raw. Instead, I shared and happily ate the rest of the glorious seafood we ordered while enjoying the pretty surroundings.

roadhouse rags

vintage store, recording studio + performance space

1600 Fortview Road
(Ben White Westbound Access)
Between Banister and Manchaca
(South East Austin) *map S26*
512.762.8797
www.myspace.com/roadhouserags

daily noon - 6p
cash only. live music

Yes. Please: *vintage > western shirts, cowboy boots, purses & jewelry, sleepwear, purdy ladies party wear, california pottery; live music*

Roadhouse Rags is a retail first for Rather. It's not only a vintage store, but also a recording studio and concert venue. I'm thinking while they're at it they should add a corn dog vendor and a ping-pong court. Okay, that's taking it a bit far, as **Roadhouse** is pretty durn perfect the way it is. What got me here was the not too big, not too small collection of vintage western wear and ladies' '50s party pretties. I was sure when I went out back to the outdoor stage there would be some couples swinging around dolled up in duds from here. There weren't, but I'll be back soon to fill the void.

schatzelein
handmade jewlry, art & accessories

1713 South 1st Street
Between Monroe and Annie
(South Austin) *map S31*
512.382.0969
http:/shop.schatzeleinaustin.com

mon - sat 11a - 6:30p sun noon - 5p
online shopping. custom designs

Yes, Please: *verabel and fox plated vintage locket, south african telephone wire bracelets, louis reith print, digby and iona emerald cut ring, gilah postcards*

Christine Fail could be an old-world screen siren: she's impossibly tall with big, expressive eyes, and she is always beautifully dressed. Fail is a modern woman also and makes everything by hand—from remodeling her home to crafting wood furniture and forging delicate pieces for her eponymous jewelry line. The delicate meets the hand-hewn at her mostly-jewelry boutique **Schatzelein**. A petite shop of indie-designer jewels makes life easy when you're hunting down a sweet gift at a modest price; you'll just be hard-pressed to leave the shop without a lovely little something for yourself. Dankeschön, Christine.

spartan

a bit of wonderul this and a bit of fantastic that

215 South Lamar #B
Near Riverside (South Austin) *map S28*
512.579.0303
www.spartan-shop.com

mon - sat 10a - 6p sun noon - 5p
online shopping. registries

Yes, Please: *japanese brass bottle openers, the wild unknown great lakes prisms, erin considine pol necklace, vintage bolivian blankets, acb aesis earrings*

I'm fully out of the closet as a lazy shopper, which you might find surprising because I shop for a living. But truth be told, I sometimes have a hard time getting myself motivated to get in my car and go out a-searchin' for a present. This is why when I find a place like **Spartan** (the neighbor to **Bows + Arrows**), I go a little cuckoo and want to buy everything in the place. There's such a brilliant array of beautifully designed and original items here that I can fill my gift coffer to the brim with loads of goodness. This way when the gift need arises I just walk back to my closet, which is a lazy shopper's dream.

stag
heritage brands for men

1423 South Congress Avenue
Corner of Elizabeth (South Austin) *map S30*
512.373.stag
www.stagaustin.com

twitter @stagaustin
mon - thu 11a - 7p fri - sat 11a - 8p
sun 11a - 6p
online shopping

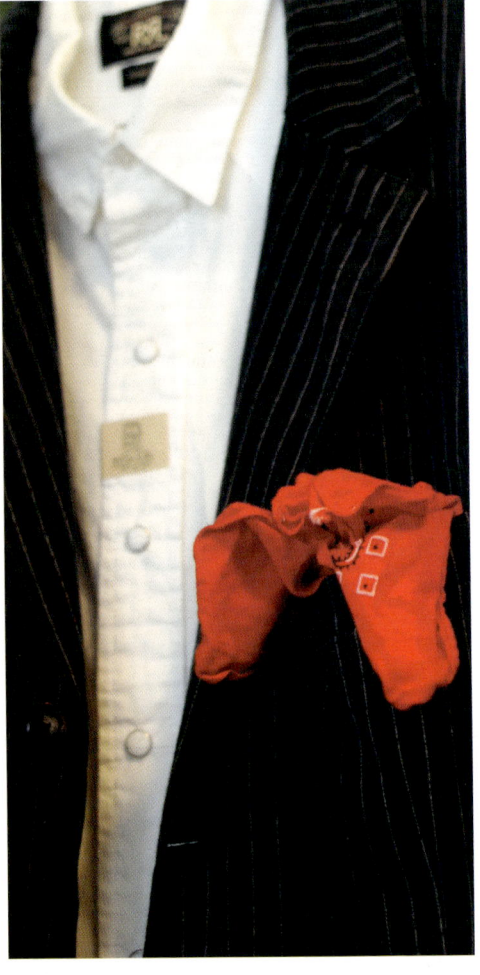

Yes, Please: *ralph lauren rrl, life after denim, oliver spencer, franklin and gower, penfield, beckel canvas, raen eyewear, vintage workboots*

The heritage tag has been applied to many things: heritage roses, heritage turkeys, heritage toys. But the biggest heritage splash might well be within the clothing industry, especially in the men's sector where heritage brands like Levi's, Pendleton and Quoddy are all the rage. An offshoot of this has been the emergence of some extraordinary retail ventures like **Stag**. It's a blast to explore here with the mix of clothing, accessories, taxidermy, found objects, and ephemera. This isn't just shopping, it's experiencing—which makes the activity all the more enjoyable.

rather.com 169

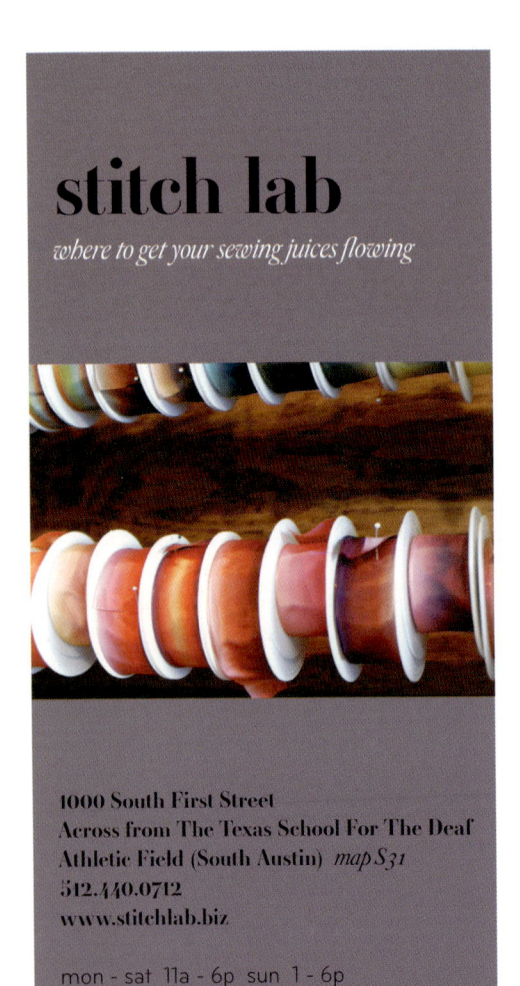

stitch lab

where to get your sewing juices flowing

**1000 South First Street
Across from The Texas School For The Deaf
Athletic Field (South Austin)** *map S31*
512.440.0712
www.stitchlab.biz

mon - sat 11a - 6p sun 1 - 6p
classes

Yes. Please: *fabrics > alexander henry, echino, moda; sublime stitching patterns, vintage figurine pin cushions, vintage deadstock zippers, classes galore*

Though the crafts of yesteryear have made a big comback recently and I know a slew of knitters and felters, many friends have secretly shared with me that sewing scares them. I understand this, as it petrifies me. Even though I come from a long line of talented sewers that includes my grandmother, mother and daughter. But **Stitch Lab**, surprisingly, didn't scare me. In fact, being here made me want to sew. From the moment I walked in and saw the cool fabrics and the cozy rooms set up with sewing machines, I felt the terror of the featherstitch disappear. Maybe I can be crafty after all.

uchi / uchiko

modern japanese cuisine

Uchi: 801 South Lamar Boulevard
Across From Juliet
Uchiko: 4200 North Lamar Boulevard
Between 42nd and 43rd
(South Austin / North Austin) *map E40*
512.916.4808
www.uchiaustin.com

twitter @uchiaustin / @uchikoaustin
sun - thu 5 - 10p fri - sat 5 - 11p
$$-$$$ reservations recommended

Yes. Please: *uchi > shiro nuta, uchi shot, omaaru ebi, chef's tasting menu; uchiko > mame yaki, wagyu momo, umaso makimono, loup crudo*

I'm not a big fan of celebrity chefs, nor do I watch The Food Network. So why do I think Tyson Cole, chef and owner of Uchi, is the bee's knees? He of Iron Chef fame, with features in every form of print media known to man? It's simple—because his food is sublime; gorgeously sourced and prepared and always interesting, making Uchi a one-of-a-kind eating experience in Austin. Wait, that is until Uchiko came along. Yes, Tyson has taken the Uchi show to the North side, and though this newly hatched spot is new to the Austin dining scene, I have no doubt it will be just as spectacular as its sibling.

rather.com

w3ll people
eco-conscious beauty products

215 South Lamar #B
Near Riverside (South Austin) *map S39*
512.366.7963
www.w3llpeople.com

twitter @w3llpeople
mon - sat 10:30a - 6p sun noon - 5p
online shopping

Yes, Please: *w3ll people cosmetics > mineral creme foundation & concealer, activist nourishing skin tonic; skin and hair care > ren, arcona, intelligent nutrients*

W3ll People makes me want to be a healthy, glowing person. But I'm finding this hard while racing around willy-nilly, throwing on random drugstore make-up so I can look like a semblance of a human being. The good folks at **W3ll People** realize this is what happens in a busy world and they have a better way. Their products are all natural, all organic and don't use the nasty fillers and yucky preservatives that's in the stuff I've been slathering on. Not only do they have their own cosmetics, they also carry a wide range of other like-minded beauty products. This is what healthy thinking looks like.

rather.com 175

whip in

a 7-eleven this is not

1950 South Ih35
Corner of Mariposa (South Austin) *map E41*
512.442.5337
www.whipin.com

twitter @whipin
daily 10a - midnight
$-$$ first come, first served

Yes, Please: *vast, eclectic collection of wine & beer, the obama shandy, egg & cheese naan with cilantro chutney, toasted panaani's*

Not to be confused with the classic Devo ditty "Whip It," the **Whip In** is a destination in Austin that's become a classic for its amazing beer and wine selection, Texas meets Gujarat-style snacks, and soooo much more. There's something in Austin's DNA that breeds convenience stores with attitude. Sure, you could come here and pick up a pack of smokes and six-pack of something cold, but you'd be missing out on what makes the **Whip In** so brilliant. I mean, what other fast stop place has live music and an in-house brewery? None I tell you.

rather.com 177

etc.

studio only, no storefronts

eat

farmhouse delivery
salt & time
smitty's

shop

alyson fox / a small collection
loretta flower
miss natalie

notes

alyson fox / a small collection

beautifully crafted simplicity

www.asmallcollection.com
www.alysonfox.com

by appointment only
online shopping. custom orders / designs.
commissions

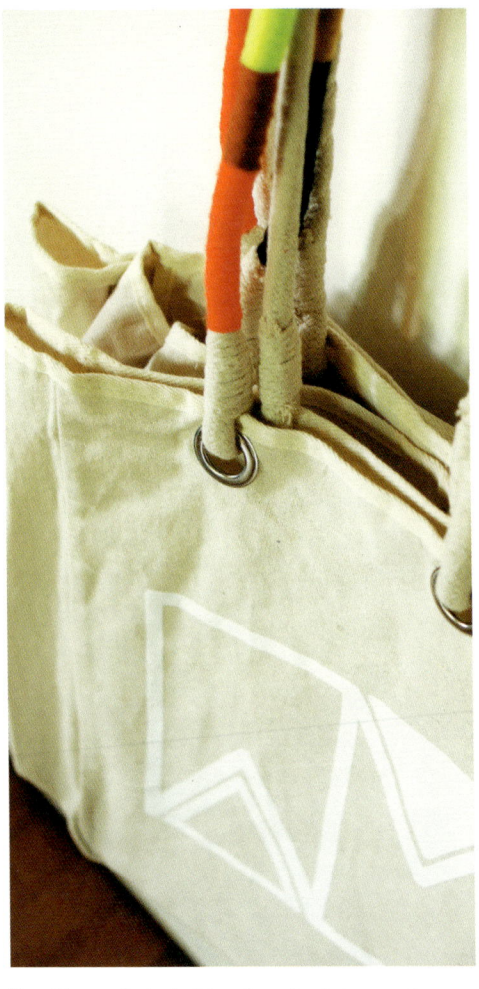

Yes, Please: *limited edition alyson fox designs > totes, raw silk silkscreen tanks, colored bead necklaces, brass spider bottle opener, dinnerware*

Alyson Fox's name was familiar, but for the life of me I couldn't connect a face to the name or even confirm that I knew Alyson. Instead of trying to figure out the puzzle, I just got on with meeting her and was struck by the multitude of talents she has. Almost everywhere I looked in her studio (and beyond) I saw something she had created. Whether it was a necklace, a photograph or a silk-screened piece of clothing, each was produced in very limited quantities. And then it came to me: I had seen her work at **Candystore Collective** in SF. The world is sometimes a very small sphere.

farmhouse delivery

delivering the farm to your door

Delivery
512.529.8569
www.farmhousedelivery.com

twitter @austinfarmhouse
weekly or bi-weekly deliveries
$$

Yes, Please: *farmhouse blend coffee, zhi tea, monk's blend black tea, paqui buttermilk tortillas, pickled dilly beans, rain lily farms herbs*

I'm a bit embarrassed to admit that I have never participated in a CSA. But before you send out the lynch mob, hear me out. I have a small family; we are no Kaie Plus 8, and we would struggle to eat a weekly ration of a dozen heads of cabbage. This is why **Farmhouse Delivery** is so brilliant. You sign up for their "farm membership" and choose weekly or biweekly home deliveries, which gets you a reasonably sized mix of produce that is grown at **Rain Lily Farm** (and elsewhere). Plus you can add meats, cheeses and other food products from carefully vetted local purveyors to your order. Sign me up!

rather.com **183**

loretta flower

a floral design studio

512.825.4789
www.lorettaflower.com

by appointment only
online shopping. custom designs.
local delivery. classes

Yes, Please: *lavender in antique medicine bottles, peonies and wildflowers in a mason jar, classes in the lovely studio, summer arrangements with succulents*

Loretta Flower is that pretty Texan lady with perfectly scuffed boots and a pearl-snap shirt who will teach you how to two-step and then knock you off your bar stool with her wit and wisdom. Loretta makes the thinking gal's floral arrangement romantic without being fussy, possessing that bountiful yet casual feel that only a floral genius can execute. Think mason jars with explosions of peonies and wildflowers. At **Loretta's** rustic Travis Heights studio, reminiscent of a floral stall in Provence, you can find owner Mary Kathryn Paynter holding classes and consultations, and she may even teach you to two-step if you ask her.

miss natalie

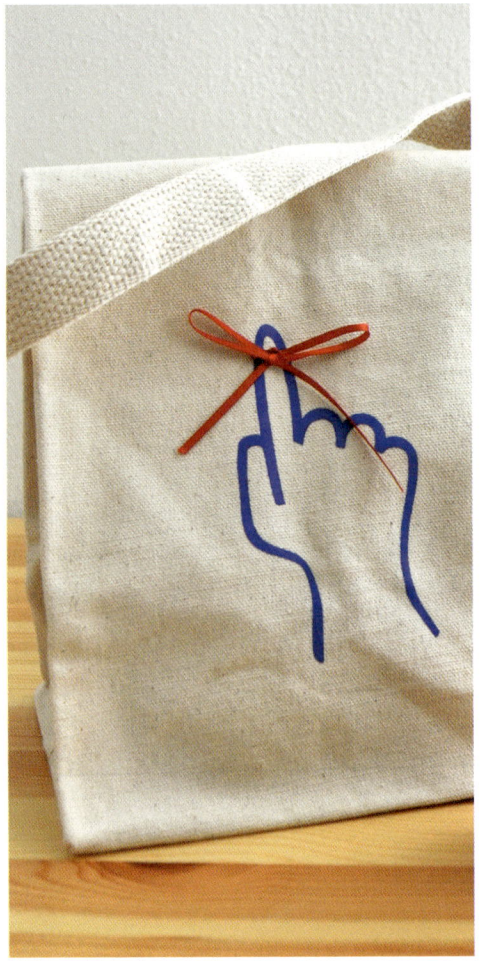

family focused handmade designs

512.983.2155
info@missnatalie.com
www.missnatalie.com

by appointment only

Yes, Please: *splendor in the snow apple box, painted hen egg, heirloom growth chart, wood burned salt box, don't forget me lunch bag*

My social set is in the throes of a baby boom, which means a calendar of baby showers and kiddie birthdays and the subsequent need for children's gifts. Thankfully, I met Natalie Davis as she was relocating to Austin from California with her charcuterie-savant husband Ben (of **Salt & Time**). Though she doesn't exclusively design for children, **Miss Natalie** has created burlap heirloom growth charts, lunch bags and wooden apple boxes that are constructed with a minimal, Scandinavian feel—tasteful standouts amongst the plastic toys and burping cloths in any mother-to-be's heap of new stuff.

salt & time

artisanal, handmade salumi and pickles

See website for Farmers Market
locations and online ordering
512.917.6071
www.saltandtime.com

twitter @saltandtime
$-$$

Yes, Please: *butcher's box subscription> salumi, genoa, sopressata, toscano, lonzino, pancetta; sour pickled cucumbers, salt cured okra, smoked pimento chile sauce*

Move over Slim Jim, there's a new game in town. Former vegan turned butcher and salumi master Ben Runkle handcrafts coppa, pancetta, prosciutto, sopressata, and more from humanely and sustainably raised meats. He starts with a whole pig, butchers it by hand, and cures, ferments and dries the meat in his Niederwald workshop. With little more than old-world techniques and a little (you guessed it) salt and time, Runkle turns out salumi worthy of an Italian butcher shop—salty, dense, and umami-rich. Visit **Salt & Time** at the Farmers' Market and create some romance Under the Tuscan Sun without ever leaving home.

rather.com

smitty's market

legendary barbeque

208 South Commerce
Between Market and Prairie Lea
(Lockhart)
512.398.9344
www.smittysmarket.com

mon - fri 7a - 6p   sat 7a - 6:30p
sun 9a - 3p
breakfast. lunch. dinner
$-$$ first come, first served

Yes, Please: *by the pound > brisket, sausage, ribs, beans; cheddar cheese, pickles, white bread*

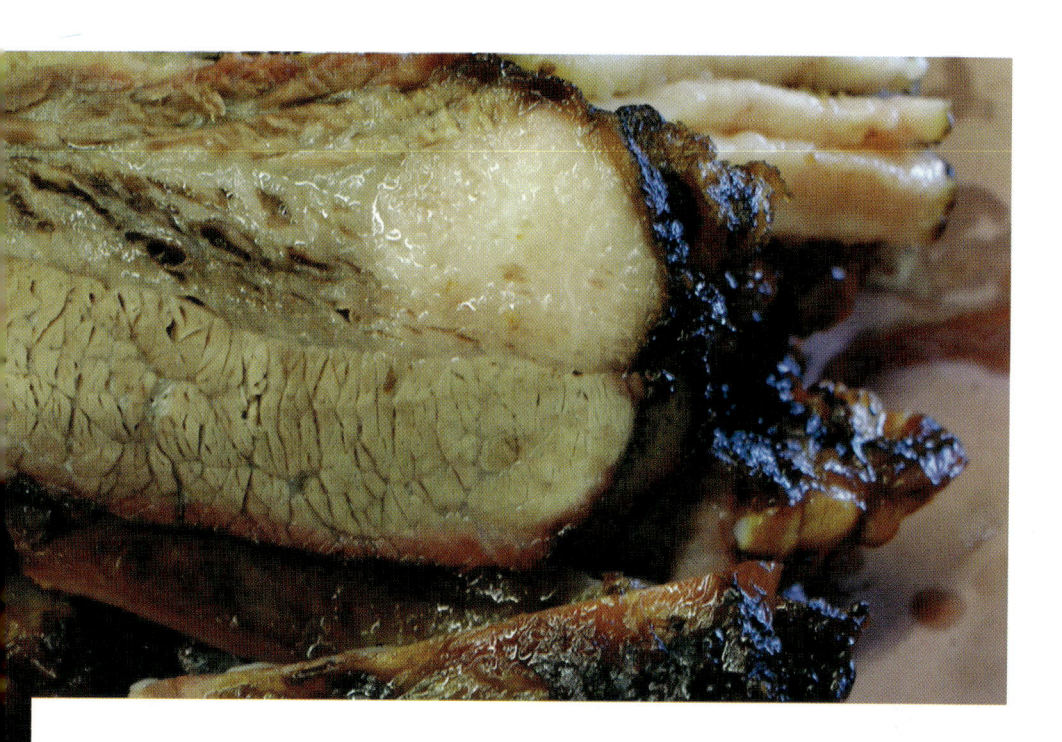

Smitty's Market is not in Austin. In fact, Lockhart, the town where **Smitty's** is located, is a fair distance from Austin, though it's often noted as being on the outskirts. So even though we usually only feature bizs in the urban core of a city, the call of **Smitty's** couldn't be resisted, with its big open fire working barbeque magic on prime pieces of Texas pork and beef. Sitting in the main room here makes you feel like Lockhart is frozen in 1968, and though there is a legendary feud that's often spoken about in conjunction to this spot, all we should care about is how ridiculously good their barbeque is.

finito

happy travels to you

rather *austin*

isbn-13 9780983314523

copyright 2011 ©swiftrank. printed in the usa

all rights reserved under international and pan-american copyright conventions. no part of this publication may be reproduced, stored in a retrieval system, or transmitted in any form or by any means, electronic, mechanical, photocopying, recording or otherwise, without prior written permission of the copyright owner.

every effort has been made to ensure the accuracy of the information in this book. however, certain details are subject to change. please remember when using the guides that hours alter seasonally and sometimes sadly, businesses close. the publisher cannot accept responsibility for any consequences arising from the use of this book.

editing / fact checking + production: chloe fields
in design master: nicole conant
map design + production: julia dickey + bryan wolf

d&a
designersandagents

thx to our friends at designers & agents for their hospitality and their support of the rather experience. please visit > designersandagents.com

rather is distributed by
independent publishers group > www.ipgbook.com

to peer further into the world of **rather** and to buy books, please visit **rather.com** to learn more